STRATEGIES FOR SUCCESS
READING

Judith Andrews Green, Director
Oxford Hills Adult Community Education
South Paris, Maine

Susan D. McClanahan
Educational Consultant

Donna D. Amstutz
Special Advisor to the Series

STECK-VAUGHN ADULT EDUCATION ADVISORY COUNCIL

Donna D. Amstutz
Asst. Project Director
Northern Area Adult Education
 Service Center
Northern Illinois University
DeKalb, Illinois

Roberta Pittman
Director, Adult Outreach Programs
 Department of Adult Education
Detroit Public Schools
Detroit, Michigan

Elaine Shelton
Consultant, Competency-Based
 Adult Education
Austin, Texas

Lonnie D. Farrell
Supervisor, Adult Special Programs
Los Angeles Unified School District
Los Angeles, California

Don F. Seaman
Professor, Adult Education
College of Education
Texas A&M University
College Station, Texas

Bobbie L. Walden
Coordinator, Community Education
Alabama Department of Education
Montgomery, Alabama

Meredyth A. Leahy
Director of Continuing
Education, Cabrini College
Radnor, Pennsylvania

Jane B. Sellen
Supervisor, Adult Education
Western Iowa Tech
 Community College
Sioux City, Iowa

STECK-VAUGHN COMPANY
AUSTIN, TEXAS
A Subsidiary of National Education Corporation

Product Design and Development: McClanahan & Company

Project Director: Larry Anger

Design/Production Director: Ellen Rongstad

Design/Production Assistant: Ed Rice

Editor: Karen Davy

Photo Research: Carrie Croton

Illustration Credits: p. 55 Peter Costa; pp. 15, 77 Laura Delano; pp. 13, 37, 39, 44, 64, 66, 99, 103 Alix Serniak.

Photo Credits: p. 11 A. Webb, Magnum Photos; p. 13 Sports Illustrated, Glamour; p. 19 Bettmann Archive; p. 20 Wide World Photos; p. 26 New York Post; p. 31 B. Anspach, Art Resource; p. 33 New York Public Library Picture Collection; p. 34 Ken Lax; p. 35 Bettmann Archive; p. 42 Ken Lax; p. 43 J. Munroe, Photo Researchers; p. 47 B. Rios, Photo Researchers; pp. 50–51 Wide World Photos; p. 52 New York Public Library Picture Collection; p. 53 Wide World Photos; p. 56 Ken Lax; p. 58 Ken Lax; p.60(l) Movie Stills Archives, (r) University of Notre Dame; p. 62 De Wys, Inc.; p. 68 H. Hammid, Photo Researchers; p. 69 De Wys, Inc.; p. 73 J. Anderson, Woodfin Camp & Assoc.; p. 74 T. Nichols, De Wys, Inc.; p. 76 Bettmann Archive; p. 77 C. Osborne, Photo Researchers; p. 90 Ken Lax; p. 95 A. Tress, Woodfin Camp & Assoc.; p. 104 Dot Pictures; p. 111 Coty; p. 117 Photo Researchers.

ISBN 0-8114-1878-2

Copyright © 1987 by Steck-Vaughn Company, Austin, Texas

2 3 4 5 6 7 8 9 0—VP 92 91 90 89 88 87

Acknowledgments

With thanks to Victoria Kimbrough for her contributions to the book, and for writing the "Strategies for Success."

And to Nora Fitzgerald for her help in the selection of the original reading passages.

Contents

To the Student

THIS BOOK AND THE GED TEST

The five sections of the GED Test measure what you know about science, mathematics, social studies, reading, and writing. This book covers one of those five areas, READING. There are four other books like this one. They cover the four other areas of study for the GED Test.

The READING part of the GED Test includes passages from newspapers, magazines, literature, and the arts. This book includes similar material. It also includes passages of interest to consumers and families.

This book is a good place to begin preparing for the GED Test. It gives you a good idea of what the test will cover. And it gives you practice in taking tests.

STRATEGIES FOR SUCCESS

In each of the five books in this series, you will find sections called *Strategies for Success*. These sections in READING, SOCIAL STUDIES, and SCIENCE will help you increase your reading power. *Strategies for Success* in WRITING and MATHEMATICS will develop your critical thinking skills.

SELF-TESTS

A Self-Test follows each lesson. The Self-Tests are designed to help you find out what you have learned. The reading passages and questions in the Self-Tests are similar to those on the GED Test. They give you an idea of what the GED Test will be like.

ANSWERS AND EXPLANATIONS

The answer keys at the end of each unit will give you the best answer for each question. For many questions, the answer key will explain why one particular answer to a question is correct, and why the other answers are wrong. These explanations provide valuable test-taking tips.

LEARNING HOW TO LEARN

There are tricks to learning and remembering. Try out different ways of learning things. Find out what ways are best for you. Here are some tips that will help you get the most out of any reading you do or any test you take.

Keep a Notebook. Writing down your thoughts about what you read may be hard at first. You may think you can't do it, or that you can't spell. Don't worry about your spelling. Your notebook is your learning tool. No one has to see it but you. You'll be surprised how interesting it will be to reread your thoughts at a later time. And you'll be surprised at how much it will help you to remember. You'll find that writing is another way of learning.

Hard Words. It isn't necessary to know every word to understand what you're reading. When you come to a hard word, don't stop. Keep on reading. The rest of the sentence or paragraph will probably help you figure out what the word means. In fact, people learn most new words that way. Use the Glossary at the end of the book to review the important words and concepts you have learned.

Understanding New Subjects. When anyone is reading about a new subject, understanding comes a little bit at a time. It's like putting together the pieces of a puzzle. When you run into something that is very hard, it's better to keep reading to the end of the paragraph or section. You can put question marks with your pencil by the parts you don't understand.

Later, reread the parts that gave you trouble. Some of the hard parts will start to make sense. Try to connect the information you are reading to the pictures and illustrations on the page. If you have a chance, talk over the hard parts with others. Don't think you have to understand everything the first time. IT'S OK TO REREAD.

Use the Study Aids in Your Book. Pay attention to what the table of contents, the unit titles, and the chapter titles can tell you about what you're learning. Also, there are explanations of important words in the margins of the pages. The pictures and illustrations often give clues about the passages you're reading. Be sure to look at them. All of these things will help you understand what you are reading.

Use the Practice Questions to Learn. Study the answers and explanations to each question in the Self-Tests. This will help you understand the passages you read.

Improve Your Test-Taking Skills. Many tests, including the GED Test, use multiple-choice questions. Each question is followed by five answers. You have to choose the BEST answer. Practice in taking tests like the ones in this book helps you to score higher on important tests like the GED.

Check What You Know

How well you do on a test doesn't always depend on how much you know about a subject. But it does depend on how well you read.

Check What You Know will give you an idea of the kind of work you will be doing in this book. It will give you an idea of how well you can find and interpret information. And it will show you which reading skills you need to improve. These skills are important in passing tests like the GED Test.

This test is very similar to the READING part of the GED Test. There are reading passages followed by one or more multiple-choice questions.

Read each passage and question carefully. Then put an X next to the BEST answer. There are a total of 20 questions. There is no time limit.

Questions 1–2 are based on the following paragraph.

At 11:40 P.M. on April 14, 1912, the luxurious ocean liner, the *Titanic*, hit an iceberg. Everyone thought that this ship was so safe it couldn't sink. Because of this, there weren't enough lifeboats for all the people on board. At 12:05 A.M. on April 15, the captain realized that the "unsinkable" ship was sinking. Only two hours later, at 2:20 in the morning, the *Titanic* disappeared into the ocean. Over 1,552 people died.

1. Why weren't there enough lifeboats on the *Titanic*?
   _____ (1) It was the largest ocean liner ever built.
   _____ (2) It was the most luxurious ocean liner ever built.
   _____ (3) Everyone thought it was so safe it couldn't sink.
   _____ (4) All of the above.
   _____ (5) None of the above.

2. The *Titanic* sank

_____ (1) two hours after it hit an iceberg.

_____ (2) two hours and forty minutes after it hit an iceberg.

_____ (3) before the captain even realized it was sinking.

_____ (4) 25 minutes after it hit an iceberg.

_____ (5) on April 14, 1912.

Questions 3–5 are based on the following table of contents.

3. This book is probably

_____ (1) a history book.

_____ (2) a novel.

_____ (3) a book that tells you how to make something.

_____ (4) a cookbook.

_____ (5) a travel book.

CONTENTS

4. If you want to know about the Mexican Revolution, which chapter would you read?

_____ (1) PLANNING YOUR TRIP

_____ (2) MEXICO'S HISTORY

_____ (3) MEXICAN FOOD AND DRINK

_____ (4) MEXICO CITY AND SURROUNDINGS

_____ (5) THE BEACHES

5. If you wanted to know about interesting places to see around Mexico City, what page would you look on?

_____ (1) 15

_____ (2) 30

_____ (3) 41

_____ (4) 59

_____ (5) 68

Questions 6–8 are based on the following paragraph.

One result of a nuclear war would be "nuclear winter." A nuclear explosion would, of course, kill many people and destroy huge amounts of property. It would also produce a lot of dust and smoke in the atmosphere. This dust and smoke in the air would block out the sun's rays. Crops and animals would freeze, and the surviving people would probably starve.

6. Which of the following would NOT be the result of
   a nuclear explosion?
   _____ (1) Many people would be killed.
   _____ (2) Huge amounts of property would be destroyed.
   _____ (3) A lot of dust and smoke would be produced.
   _____ (4) Most crops and animals would survive.
   _____ (5) The sun's rays would be blocked.

7. The "atmosphere" is
   _____ (1) the air.
   _____ (2) dust and smoke.
   _____ (3) the sun's rays.
   _____ (4) crops and animals.
   _____ (5) none of the above.

8. From the information in this paragraph, you can
   conclude that a nuclear explosion would
   _____ (1) cause the world to get hotter.
   _____ (2) cause the world to get colder.
   _____ (3) not affect the temperature of the world.
   _____ (4) cause the sun to freeze.
   _____ (5) none of the above.

Questions 9–10 are based on the following passage.

A limerick is a short poem. All limericks have the same number of lines, and they all rhyme in the same way. Look at this example:

There was a young lady named Lynn,
Who was so unbelievably thin
That when she essayed
To drink lemonade,
She slipped through the straw and fell in.

9. From this passage, you can conclude that all limericks
_____ (1) have five lines.
_____ (2) are about women.
_____ (3) have very long lines.
_____ (4) all of the above.
_____ (5) none of the above.

10. Look at the different meanings for *essay* in the dictionary. Which of these meanings does the word have in the limerick?
_____ (1) to test the nature or quality of something
_____ (2) to try
_____ (3) a trial
_____ (4) a short piece of writing
_____ (5) none of the above

essay vt. (e sá́) 1. to test the nature or quality of something 2. to try —**n.** (é sā) 1. a trial 2. a short piece of writing

Questions 11–12 are based on the following article.

WHAT ARE YOUR CHANCES OF BEING AN OLD MAID?

A recent study said that college-educated white women who haven't married by their 25th birthday have only a 50% chance of getting married. (The chances are higher for white women with no higher education.) If a woman hasn't gotten married by 30, she has only a 20% chance of ever doing so. By 35, her chances have dropped to 5%. Only 1% of unmarried college-educated white women aged 40 will ever tie the knot.

11. What is the main idea of this article?

_____ (1) Most white women are college educated.

_____ (2) All women should try to go to college.

_____ (3) Younger women make better wives.

_____ (4) It's better for people to get married when they're young.

_____ (5) The older a woman gets, the less chance she has of getting married.

12. In this article, "tie the knot" probably means

_____ (1) to get married.

_____ (2) to go to college.

_____ (3) to tie a piece of string in a knot.

_____ (4) to get divorced.

_____ (5) to get younger.

Questions 13–15 are based on the following paragraph.

In recent years, people have begun to understand how important it is to eat fiber. Eating a lot of whole grains, dried beans, fruits, and vegetables can help prevent intestinal problems such as constipation, hemorrhoids, and even colon cancer. Eating foods high in fiber can also reduce the amount of cholesterol in the blood.

13. What is the main idea of this paragraph?

_____ (1) Constipation, hemorrhoids, and colon cancer are intestinal problems.

_____ (2) It's important to eat foods that contain fiber.

_____ (3) Eating whole grains can help prevent colon cancer.

_____ (4) Cholesterol is often found in the blood.

_____ (5) None of the above.

14. The "colon" is probably

    ____ (1) a disease.

    ____ (2) a kind of fruit.

    ____ (3) part of the intestines.

    ____ (4) something that you find in blood.

    ____ (5) a kind of fiber.

15. From the information in this paragraph, you can infer that whole grains, dried beans, fruits, and vegetables

    ____ (1) are foods that contain a lot of fiber.

    ____ (2) are foods we should eat.

    ____ (3) help reduce cholesterol in the blood.

    ____ (4) all of the above.

    ____ (5) none of the above.

Questions 16–18 are based on the following letter.

To the Editor:

    When our mayor was elected to office two years ago, he promised to clean up the city government and get rid of all the corrupt officials. Not one person has lost his or her job since the mayor took office! There is evidence that at least five officials have been taking bribes and mishandling city money for years. But the mayor does nothing. He has let the citizens of this city down. Could it be that he's a crook too? Keep this in mind when you vote for mayor in next month's election!

---

16. What is the main idea of this letter?

    ____ (1) Five officials are taking bribes.

    ____ (2) City money is being mishandled.

    ____ (3) The mayor isn't keeping his promise to clean up the city government.

    ____ (4) The mayor has already been in office two years.

    ____ (5) Everyone should vote in the election for mayor next month.

17. The writer says there is evidence that five city officials broke the law.   What did they do wrong?

_____ (1) They corrupted other officials.

_____ (2) They took bribes.

_____ (3) They mishandled the elections.

_____ (4) They mishandled city money.

_____ (5) Both 2 and 4.

18. The writer of the letter probably

_____ (1) thinks the mayor is doing a terrible job fighting corruption.

_____ (2) has no strong feelings about the mayor.

_____ (3) is angry with the mayor.

_____ (4) is a good friend of the mayor.

_____ (5) both 1 and 3.

Questions 19–20 are based on the following review.

MOVIE CLASSICS

The African Queen (1951) may be old, but it is fabulous from start to finish.   Katharine Hepburn sparkles as always, and Humphrey Bogart is a winner.   If you haven't seen it, don't miss it.   If you have, try it again!

19. The main idea of this movie review is

_____ (1) *The African Queen* is a very good movie.

_____ (2) Katharine Hepburn always sparkles.

_____ (3) Humphrey Bogart is a winner.

_____ (4) *The African Queen* is old.

_____ (5) none of the above.

20. The writer

_____ (1) thinks the movie is very good.

_____ (2) likes both Hepburn and Bogart in the movie.

_____ (3) likes Hepburn, but doesn't like Bogart in the movie.

_____ (4) both 1 and 2.

_____ (5) both 2 and 3.

Compare your answers with those in *Answers and Explanations* on page 9. Then complete the chart below by checking the numbers of the questions you got wrong.

SKILL PREVIEW CHART

The chart will show you which reading skills you need to pay special attention to. Reread each question you got wrong. Then look at the appropriate sections of the book for help in figuring out the right answers.

SKILLS	TEST QUESTIONS	STRATEGIES FOR SUCCESS
The test, like this book, focuses on the skills below.	Check (✔) the questions you got wrong.	Preview what you will learn in this book. Learn how to get the right answers.
Finding Information Quickly and Efficiently	___ 3 ___ 4 ___ 5 ___ 17	See pages 26–27 **STRATEGIES FOR SUCCESS** • Predicting • Scanning
Getting the Meaning of Words from Context	___ 7 ___ 10 ___ 12 ___ 14	See pages 42–43 **STRATEGIES FOR SUCCESS** • Getting Meaning from Context
Understanding the Main Idea	___ 13 ___ 16 ___ 19	See pages 68–69 **STRATEGIES FOR SUCCESS** • The Topic Sentence • The Unstated Main Idea
Understanding the Organization of a Paragraph	___ 2 ___ 1 ___ 6 ___ 11	See pages 90–91 **STRATEGIES FOR SUCCESS** • Chronological Order • Comparison and Contrast • Cause and Effect • Examples
Correctly Interpreting What You Read	___ 8 ___ 9 ___ 15 ___ 18 ___ 20	See pages 116–117 **STRATEGIES FOR SUCCESS** • Making Inferences • Drawing Conclusions • Fact and Opinion

Answers and Explanations

1. (3) The phrase "because of this" tells you that there weren't enough lifeboats because everyone thought the *Titanic* was so safe.

2. (2) The time expressions tell you that the ship first hit the iceberg at 11:40 P.M. on April 14 and it disappeared, or sank, at 2:20 A.M. on April 15. So it sank two hours and forty minutes after it hit an iceberg.

3. (5) All the chapter titles are about a foreign country, Mexico. The second chapter talks about planning a trip. From this, you can guess that this is a travel book.

4. (2) The Mexican Revolution is part of Mexico's history.

5. (5) "Surroundings" are places that are nearby. So the chapter on page 68 would tell you about things to see near Mexico City.

6. (4) The crops and animals would not survive because they would freeze and die.

7. (1) If a bomb exploded, dust and smoke would go up into the air around the earth. So you can infer that "atmosphere" is the air.

8. (2) If plants and animals would freeze, you can conclude that a nuclear explosion would make the world colder.

9. (1) The writer tells you that all limericks have the same number of lines. The limerick in the passage has five lines. So you know that all limericks have five lines.

10. (2) From the context of the poem, you know that Lynn isn't testing the quality of the lemonade. She's just trying to drink it with a straw.

11. (5) The whole article explains why older women have less chance of getting married than younger women.

12. (1) The whole article talks about the chances of a woman getting married at different ages. The last sentence gives the same kind of information as all the other sentences. It just uses a different expression to say "get married."

13. (2) All the other answers are about things that are mentioned in the paragraph. But only (2) gives the general idea of the whole paragraph. The other answers are too limited.

14. (3) The words *such as* tell you that constipation, hemorrhoids, and colon cancer are all examples of intestinal problems.

15. (4) The first sentence says eating fiber is important. Then the writer mentions some foods that help prevent some illnesses. You can infer that the foods mentioned contain fiber. If they prevent illnesses, we should eat them. And if they're high in fiber, then they will reduce cholesterol in the blood.

16. (3) All the other answers are about things that are mentioned in the paragraph. But only (3) gives the general idea of the whole paragraph. The other answers are too limited.

17. (5) If you scan the paragraph for the word *evidence*, you find it in the third sentence. Following that word, you see that the officials took bribes and mishandled city money.

18. (5) The writer obviously has strong feelings about the mayor—she's angry with him. She says that the mayor has let the people of the city down. That is, she thinks he isn't doing his job.

19. (1) The writer talks about (2), (3), and (4), but his main idea is that the movie is good. The ideas in (2) and (3) help explain why the movie is good. But they are too limited to be the main idea.

20. (4) The writer says "don't miss it." So he likes the movie. He says that Hepburn "sparkles" and Bogart is "a winner." So you know he likes both of them.

FINDING INFORMATION

THERE are many skills that you can develop to make you a better reader. Two of these are predicting and scanning. If you can predict what a reading passage is about, you can decide quickly whether or not you need to read it—or want to read it.

Scanning lets you pick out just the information that you need from a passage without reading the whole thing. Scanning helps you find facts quickly and efficiently.

1. PREDICTING

WE **predict** things every day of our lives. Imagine one evening you look out the window, and you see snow falling. A little later the weatherman on TV says it's going to snow all night and the temperature will stay in the teens. You can guess, or predict, what the roads will be like the next morning— icy and dangerous. It's obvious that being able to predict this is helpful. If you have to drive to work or school, you know you should start earlier than usual. If your car doesn't have snow tires, you know you had better get some quickly. If there is some other, safer way to get to work or school, you know that tomorrow would be a good day to take it.

Let's look at another example of how predicting can be helpful. Imagine you want to go to a movie. You open the newspaper, and you see this ad.

Is this a romantic movie? A comedy? A war movie? Science fiction? It isn't hard to predict what the movie is about. If you hate violence, you have a pretty good idea that you wouldn't like this movie.

Predicting can help you in your reading too. Suppose you are looking for a **specific** kind of information. For example, suppose you want to buy the best car you can for under $9,000. Which of these magazines would you look in?

From the picture on the cover and the title, you can guess that *Consumer World* would be your best bet.

Now look at the **table of contents** below. You still want to find out about cars under $9,000. Can you predict from the title which **article** you should turn to?

TABLE OF CONTENTS. A list of the articles in a magazine or chapters in a book.

ARTICLE. A complete piece of writing in a magazine or newspaper.

You should probably turn to page 85. But what if you're not sure whether a $9,000 car is a medium-priced car or an economy car? Often the first few sentences of an article give you a general idea of what the whole article is going to be about. By reading just those sentences, you can usually decide if the information you want is going to be in the article or not. For example, look at the first sentences from two of the articles in *Consumer World:*

Our Choice in Economy Cars

There are several outstanding cars in the economy class division, $4,900–$9,000.

The Best in Medium-Priced Cars

Twenty medium-priced cars, ranging from $10,000–$15,000, have been tested.

It's obvious that you should read the article on the left for the information you want.

Likewise, if you're looking for information in a book, the table of contents will often give you an idea of the information the **chapter** contains. If not, the first few sentences of a chapter often tell you what the chapter is about.

Look at the table of contents from *Keeping Healthy.* If you want to know whether or not a certain drug is harmful to your body, which chapter should you read?

CHAPTER. A book is often divided into several parts, or chapters.

You probably predicted that you would find out about drugs in Chapter 8. Maybe you knew that *narcotics* is another name for drugs. Or maybe you decided that tobacco and alcohol are similar to drugs, and thought the information would be in Chapter 8.

Most of the chapter titles in *Keeping Healthy* give you an idea of what kind of information you can find in the chapter. But what about Chapter 7? What do you think it's about? If you don't know, you can turn to the first page and read the first few sentences. They will probably tell you. Look at the beginning of Chapter 7.

7. CONTROL OF THE BODY

INTRODUCTION

The human body is very complicated. Every part has a special job to do, and yet all the parts work together to make the body efficient. They are able to do this because the nervous system controls and regulates all the different parts and all the different activities of the body.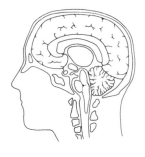

Now you can be pretty sure that this chapter is going to be about the nervous system. From the picture, you know that the chapter is also going to tell you about the brain. You might also guess, or predict, that the brain is a part of the nervous system. You have made an **educated guess**, a prediction, about the contents of the chapter.

EDUCATED GUESS. A guess that you make based on your knowledge and experience.

$\mathcal{S}$elf-Test

Answer the questions. Then compare your answers with those in *Answers and Explanations* on page 28.

Put an X next to the best answer.

1. You want to know what to do if you burn yourself with boiling water. In which of the following books would you find the information?
   _____ (1) *Home Accidents—What to Do in an Emergency*
   _____ (2) *A Healthy and More Beautiful You*
   _____ (3) *Safety Tips from the American Health Association*
   _____ (4) *Injuries on the Playing Field*
   _____ (5) Both 1 and 3

2. Look at the following headlines. Which of these newspaper articles would you read if you were interested in new laws concerning tenants and landlords?

   _____ (1) **Gonzalez Plans to Build 5 New Apartment Buildings**

   _____ (2) **Very Few Empty Apartments Left in the City**

   _____ (3) *Landlords Against New Rent Control Laws*

   _____ (4) **Apartment Workers' Union Goes on Strike**

   _____ (5) **LOOKING FOR A GOOD PLACE TO LIVE**

3. Which of the articles in number 2 above would you probably read if you wanted to move to a new apartment?
   _____ (1) Articles 1 and 2
   _____ (2) Articles 3 and 4
   _____ (3) Article 5
   _____ (4) Articles 1 and 5
   _____ (5) All of the above

16

4. Here are the tables of contents from two books.

1.

TABLE OF CONTENTS	Page
Pipes, drains, and leaky faucets	4
Wires and switches	35
When the toaster won't pop	50
Getting ready to paint	98
Hints for a smooth coat	122

2.

TABLE OF CONTENTS	Page
You and Your Spouse	2
You and Your Landlord	40
You and Your Business	79
You and Your Property	101
You and Public Assistance	132

Write the number of the book and the name of the chapter where you would find the following information.

Information	Book	Chapter
what to do if you want a divorce	2	You and Your Spouse
what to do if the toilet is stopped up	___	_____
what to do if all the lights go out	___	_____
what to do if you are renting an apartment and get an eviction notice	___	_____

2. SCANNING

OFTEN when you read, you're looking for specific information. You may not have time or you may not want to read a whole article, chapter, or **passage.** The truth is you probably don't have to read everything. You can run your eyes quickly over the words and just look for the information you need. This is called **scanning.** Suppose you are looking at newspaper ads for an apartment. You know you can't spend more than $400 a month. The only ads you need to read are the ones for apartments under $400. You can ignore all the others. Look at this page from the Classified Ads. Which ads would you read? Check (✔) the ones for apartments under $400.

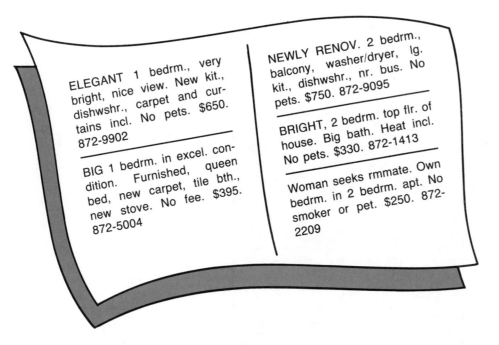

ELEGANT 1 bedrm., very bright, nice view. New kit., dishwshr., carpet and curtains incl. No pets. $650. 872-9902

BIG 1 bedrm. in excel. condition. Furnished, queen bed, new carpet, tile bth., new stove. No fee. $395. 872-5004

NEWLY RENOV. 2 bedrm., balcony, washer/dryer, lg. kit., dishwshr., nr. bus. No pets. $750. 872-9095

BRIGHT, 2 bedrm. top flr. of house. Big bath. Heat incl. No pets. $330. 872-1413

Woman seeks rmmate. Own bedrm. in 2 bedrm. apt. No smoker or pet. $250. 872-2209

When you were deciding which ads to check, did you read every ad completely? Or did you just run your eyes down the page and look for a dollar sign ($) and the numbers after it? To get the information you needed, that's all you had to do.

Take another example. Let's say you know that the following **paragraph** is about Andrew Jackson. But you don't know where he was from. You need to find out one piece of information: the state Jackson came from. How would you go about finding this information?

The first truly democratic President of the United States was Andrew Jackson. He came from the state of Tennessee, which still didn't have very many people and was not considered very civilized. Most of the old politicians were upset when he was elected, and even a little afraid. They considered him somewhat of a woodsman, a barbarian, which is how they saw most people from the "frontier" states like Tennessee, Kentucky, and Ohio.

You know that the names of places are usually **capitalized**. You can scan the paragraph and look only at the words that begin with a capital letter. The first words with capital letters are *President* and *United States*, but you know these words aren't the name of a state. Then you see *Andrew Jackson*, but that's a person's name, not a state. Then your eyes jump to *Tennessee*. It is the name of a state. So you stop and read a few words before and a few words after the word *Tennessee* to see if that's where Jackson came from. If it is, you can stop reading right there. In other words, you don't have to read the whole paragraph.

Like the word *Tennessee*, some kinds of information are easier to find than others. It is easier to find a **proper name**—the name of a person, business, city, state, or country—than it is to find a word like *happy*. Titles are easy to find because they are capitalized, and they are usually italicized. Numbers are easy to find too. If you need to find a date, you know it will look something like this: December 14, 1950, or like this: 12/14/50. Dates stand out from the words around them. So do telephone numbers, which are usually seven numbers (ten with the area code). Addresses are also easy to find because they are always written in a **predictable** way.

Read the following questions. Then try to find the answers in the passage below WITHOUT reading the whole passage.
1. How long has Baryshnikov been in the United States?
2. What is the name of his new movie?
3. What does Baryshnikov do besides make movies?

PROPER NAME. A name used for one particular person or thing. A proper name always begins with a capital letter.

PREDICTABLE. When you can guess or describe something in advance because you have information about it.

Mikhail Baryshnikov has been in the United States only 10 years, and he has already become not only the most famous dancer in the country, but also a new, and apparently very talented, movie star. His new film *White Nights* is being acclaimed all over the country, and Mr. Baryshnikov has become an overnight star.

The film, which in many ways parallels Baryshnikov's own life, is about a Russian ballet dancer who defects to the United States. He finds himself in Russia again a few years later because of a plane crash. He meets an American

If you are taking a test, and the answer to a question has a predictable form, you can probably find it easily and quickly without reading everything in a passage. You could answer the first question easily because you only had to find a number (10). You could answer the second question quickly because you had to find a proper name or title *(White Nights)*.

But what if the answer you are looking for doesn't stand out? Do you have to read the whole passage? Not necessarily. Often you can concentrate on looking for one or two words. For example, to answer question number 3 about Baryshnikov, you knew you needed a word that meant a profession, an occupation, or an activity. As your eyes scanned the sentences, you could quickly pass over words that didn't have this meaning. You could look only for the kind of word you wanted. In this case, you found an occupation (dancer).

Sometimes the test question will tell you what kind of word you should look for in a passage. For example, look at this question:

Circle the best answer.
Cotton seeds are used to make

    a. sheets.

    b. oil.

    c. lint.

    d. fiber.

    e. clothing.

To find the answer in the paragraph on the next page, what word would you look for? Probably *seed.* So you would be looking for a short word with two *ee*'s in it, and you can skip over all the long ones.

Cotton is a fiber. It is used all over the world to make clothing and many other things that we use daily like towels, sheets, and bags. A use has been found for every part of the cotton boll. The seeds are used to make oil. The meal that is left after the oil has been extracted can be used to feed livestock. Even the lint is gathered and used to make textiles.

Once you find the word you want, you can check for the answer to the question. To do this, read some of the words before the word *seed* or some of the words after it to find the information that matches one of the answers.

FOR YOUR INFORMATION

On a test, you often have a reading passage, followed by several questions—like the ones in the Self-Tests in this book. There may be words in the passage that you don't understand. But that's no reason to panic. You may be able to answer the questions even if you don't understand every word. For example, in the paragraph about cotton, you could answer the question without understanding *boll, extracted, livestock,* or *textile.*

$\mathcal{S}$elf-Test

Answer the questions. Then compare your answers with those in *Answers and Explanations* on page 29.

Questions 1–3 are based on the label from a can of disinfectant.

1. Read the instructions. Imagine that there is something you don't like about the product. Where would you write to complain?

   _____

   _____

   _____

Put an X next to the best answer.

2. When you were looking for the information in question 1, you probably knew you had to find

   _____ (1) a telephone number.

   _____ (2) a date.

   _____ (3) a person's name.

   _____ (4) the name of a business.

   _____ (5) the name of a business and an address.

3. Imagine you just got some of the disinfectant in your eyes, and you want to know what to do. You would read the paragraph that begins with the word or words

   _____ (1) Flammable

   _____ (2) First Aid

   _____ (3) Warning

   _____ (4) To disinfect

   _____ (5) Do not use

Warning: Avoid contact with food. Avoid spraying into eyes.

Flammable! Contents are under pressure. Do not use near flame or fire. Do not puncture or incinerate container.

First Aid: If sprayed into eyes, immediately flush with plenty of cool water. Get medical attention if irritation continues.

To disinfect:
1. Hold can upright 8″ to 10″ from surface.
2. Spray surface 2 to 3 seconds until covered.
Do not use on wood furniture or acrylic plastics.

Lavalle Household Products
293 Bloomfield Ave.
Montclair, New Jersey 07043

Made in U.S.A.

23

Many famous people have been physically handicapped; they have been blind or deaf or had lost an arm or leg. Ludwig van Beethoven, the famous composer, became partially deaf at 32 and totally deaf at 46. But he continued to produce great music. French actress Sarah Bernhardt had her leg amputated in 1914. But she continued to perform on the stage until her death in 1923. Helen Keller was both blind and deaf from the age of two. But she became a famous lecturer and wrote ten books. Franklin D. Roosevelt became President of the United States after both his legs were paralyzed from polio. And Henri de Toulouse-Lautrec, the French impressionist painter, fell when he was 14. He never grew to normal height.

4. Which person in this paragraph had more than one handicap?
   _____ (1) Ludwig van Beethoven
   _____ (2) Henri de Toulouse-Lautrec
   _____ (3) Franklin D. Roosevelt
   _____ (4) Helen Keller
   _____ (5) Sarah Bernhardt

5. How many people did you read about before you found the answer to question 4?
   _____ (1) One
   _____ (2) Two
   _____ (3) Three
   _____ (4) Four
   _____ (5) Five

Question 6 is based on the following paragraph. First read the question. Scan the paragraph to find the answer as quickly as possible.

All electric wires in your home are insulated. The color of the insulation tells you what kind of wire it is. If the insulation around a wire is white, you are looking at a neutral wire, that is, one that has no electricity running to it. If the wire is red, blue, or black, it is a hot wire. It receives electric current and is dangerous. Gray or green wires are ground wires. They, like the white wires, do not receive electric current.

6. What color(s) are dangerous wires?
_____ (1) White
_____ (2) Red only
_____ (3) Green only
_____ (4) Red, blue, and black
_____ (5) Gray and green

THINKING AND WRITING

1. Look at the paragraph about famous people on page 24. Find the sentence that tells what Sarah Berhardt did for a living and write it here.

_____

_____

2. Look at the ads on page 18. Find an ad for an apartment where you can probably have pets. Use the information in the ad and write a short paragraph describing the apartment.

_____

_____

_____

Compare your answers with those in *Answers and Explanations* on page 30.

STRATEGIES FOR SUCCESS

1. PREDICTING

There are certain parts of a reading passage that can help you predict what the passage is about.

STRATEGY: Look at the title or first few sentences.

1. Read the title, headline, chapter name, or first few lines of a passage.
2. Use your logic to figure out what a passage is about.

Example: What do you think this newspaper article is about?

> Tragedy struck this morning just before noon. Seventy-two seconds after the space shuttle took off, it exploded in a huge ball of fire. All seven astronauts were killed including teacher Christa McAuliffe, the first civilian ever chosen to go into space.

These first few sentences give you the facts about the explosion of the space shuttle. From this you can guess that the rest of the article will be about the accident: what happened, why it happened, and who was involved.

Write: What do you think this magazine article is about? Write your answer. Use the strategy above.

So You're Going to Have a Baby—Alone

_____

_____

2. SCANNING

Scanning helps you find specific information quickly without reading every word.

STRATEGY: Think about the form of the information.

1. Decide if you're looking for a number, a date, a proper name, a short word, etc.
2. Run your eyes through the passage and look for the piece of information.
3. Check the other words in the sentence to be sure you have the right piece of information.

Example: Scan this paragraph and find the name of the person who was President in 1956. Then stop reading.

> If it weren't for a dog, Richard Nixon might never have been President. Eisenhower, the President in 1956, was thinking of replacing Nixon as Vice-President. In a very emotional speech to the people of the U.S., Nixon tried to show that he was an honest, capable man. In the speech he mentioned his dog, Checkers. He said he would never give Checkers up. People were moved by this loyalty to a pet, and they believed that Nixon was honest. Eisenhower kept him on as Vice-President.

You need to look for the date, 1956. When you find it, you see that the information around it tells you that Eisenhower was President that year. So this is the last sentence you have to read.

Write: Scan the paragraph again, and find the name of Nixon's dog. Write the last sentence you had to read. Use the strategy above.

Compare your answers with those in *Answers and Explanations* on page 30.

Answers and Explanations

1. PREDICTING

1. (5) Number 2 is not a book about accidents. Number 4 is about accidents, but accidents linked to sports. Number 1 is about home accidents, so you would almost certainly find information about burns there. Number 3 gives safety hints in general, so it would probably tell you what to do for burns too.

2. (3) All of the articles are about apartments. But number 3 is the only one about a new law concerning tenants and landlords.

3. (5) All of these articles give you some kind of information about apartments and how to find a place to live.

4.

Information	Book	Chapter
what to do if you want a divorce	2	**You and Your Spouse**
what to do if the toilet is stopped up	1	**Pipes, drains, and leaky faucets**
what to do if all the lights go out	1	**Wires and switches**
what to do if you are renting an apartment and get an eviction notice	2	**You and Your Landlord**

2 — You and Your Spouse

Book 2 tells about laws and civil rights. The chapter "You and Your Spouse" probably tells about divorce because *spouse* means "husband or wife."

1 — Pipes, drains, and leaky faucets

Book 1 tells about things that need to be fixed. The chapter "Pipes, drains, and leaky faucets" probably tells you how to fix a toilet because it's in the bathroom and uses water like the other things mentioned.

1 — Wires and switches

Book 1 is the only book about how to fix things. The chapter "Wires and switches" probably tells about electrical problems.

2 — You and Your Landlord

Book 2 is the only book that tells about laws and civil rights. The chapter "You and Your Landlord" probably tells you how to solve problems with your landlord.

2. SCANNING

1.   Lavalle Household Products
       293 Bloomfield Ave.
       Montclair, New Jersey 07043

2. (5) If you're going to write to complain, you need the name of a company and an address. You would scan for a group of words that looked like a name and address.

3. (2) If you do something wrong, like get the product in your eye, look under *First Aid* to find out what to do. Under *Warning, Flammable,* and *Do Not Use . . .* , you are usually told all the things you should NOT do with the product. *To disinfect* tells you how to use the product.

4. (4) Scan for names. Then read the words before or after each name to see how many handicaps each person had.

5. (3) There is only one person in the paragraph who had more than one handicap. When you read that Helen Keller was both blind and deaf, you can stop reading.

6. (4) is the correct answer. You had to scan for the word *wire* or *dangerous*, or for one of the colors.

THINKING AND WRITING

1.   French actress Sarah Bernhardt had her leg amputated in 1914.

Scan the paragraph until you find the name *Sarah Bernhardt,* and then read the information around the name.

2.   It is a big one-bedroom apartment in excellent condition. It is furnished, and there is a queen-size bed and new carpet. There is also a tile bathroom and a new stove in the kitchen.

STRATEGIES FOR SUCCESS

1. Predicting

The article is probably about having a child when you aren't married.

2. Scanning

Checkers. In the speech he mentioned his dog, Checkers.

THE MEANING OF WORDS

WHAT do you do when you're reading and you find a word that you don't understand? You could look up every word in a dictionary. But you don't always need to know the exact meaning of a word. Also, if you had to look up every word, you probably wouldn't have the patience to read for very long. Fortunately, you can often guess what a word means by looking at the other words around it. This unit will show you how to figure out what words mean.

GETTING MEANING FROM CONTEXT

WHEN you are reading, you often come to a word that you don't understand. How can you find out what the word means? If the word were all alone, it would be very difficult. For example, what do you think this word means?

aquarium

Is it a thing? Is it a person? Is it an animal? Is it a kind of car? Read the following passage and see if you can guess what *aquarium* means.

STARTING YOUR OWN AQUARIUM

You can make an interesting aquarium for very little money. First put some clean sand in the bottom of a glass tank. Then get some ordinary water plants and push them into the sand. Fill the tank carefully with tap water and put it on a sunny windowsill. When the water has cleared and the plants have begun to grow, put in some small fish. Now you can sit back and watch a whole new world live and grow.

Now you have some help to figure out the meaning of *aquarium*. *Aquarium* has a lot of other words around it. It is in a **context**. And from the context, we know that an aquarium is a glass tank that contains sand, water, plants, and fish. We also know that the plants and fish are alive. In other words, you don't have to look up the word *aquarium* in the dictionary. You can figure out what it means by using the context.

CONTEXT. The parts of a sentence or a paragraph that help you figure out the meaning of a word.

Now look at this passage about a day at the San Diego Zoo. What do you think *aviary* means?

After looking at the monkeys, we decided to find the birds. We saw a big sign that said AVIARY, so we headed in that direction. When we got to the aviary, I was astounded. It was huge, and there must have been two hundred different kinds of birds inside. This was the tropical aviary. So it looked like a jungle, and the birds were every color of the rainbow.

You may not know the exact **definition** of the word *aviary*. You may not know what it is made of or exactly how it looks. But since you know you are at a zoo, and the aviary is full of birds, you can guess that it must be the place where they keep birds at a zoo.

DEFINITION. Words or a sentence that give the exact meaning of a word.

In both of the paragraphs above, you figured out the meaning of the words from the other information in the paragraph. But sometimes, the writer will actually give you the definition of a word.

No one really knows how long man has been on earth. Some people say 1,000,000 years. Some people say 4,000,000, depending on how they define "man." However, we know that homo sapiens, the first people on earth who were physically similar to men and women today, have existed for only about 40,000 or 50,000 years.

You don't have to look up the words *homo sapien* in the dictionary. Just read a little farther and you can find out what they mean. Often a **comma** after a word tells you that more information about the word is going to follow. In the paragraph on the preceding page, *homo sapiens* is followed by the information "the first people on earth who were physically similar to men and women today."

Here is another example of a definition that follows a comma.

When you write, you usually don't want to use the same words over and over again. To avoid repeating a word, you often use a synonym, a word that means the same or almost the same as another word. For example, a synonym for *want* is *would like*. Some synonyms for *pretty* are *attractive* and *good-looking*. When you look up a word in a dictionary, you often find synonyms as well as a definition. Another book where you can find synonyms is called a thesaurus.

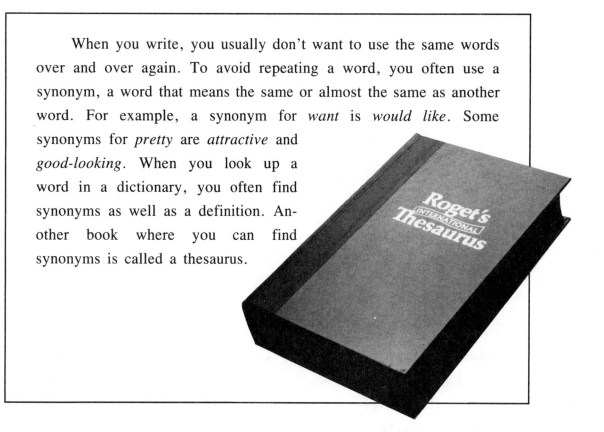

In this paragraph, you have the definition of two words. They are *synonym* and *thesaurus*. The definition of *synonym* comes after a comma. A synonym is a word that means the same or almost the same as another word. The definition of *thesaurus* comes before the word. It is a book where you can find synonyms.

Often a writer will give you examples that help you understand what a word means. Look at this ad. What do you think *small appliance* means?

From the examples, you know that small appliances are all the small electric machines that you use around the house.

Writers sometimes show you when they are going to give you examples or definitions. They might use a comma, a dash (—), or a colon (:) before the examples. Or they might use words like *such as*, *like*, or *for example*. Look at these examples.

In the 19th century, the world saw many new inventions: photography (1839), the typewriter (1867), the telephone (1876), the electric light (1879), the automobile (1887), and motion pictures (1894).

All the rings that she makes are in geometrical designs like triangles, circles, squares, and rectangles.

In the first sentence, you can guess what *invention* means from the examples and dates following the colon. You can guess that the telephone did not exist before 1876 or the electric light before 1879. So an invention is something that someone makes that did not exist before.

In the second sentence, examples of geometrical designs follow the word *like*. So you know that a geometrical design is a circle, a square, and so on.

Sometimes you can guess what a word means because you are told what the word DOESN'T mean. Look at this paragraph. What do you think *extrovert* means? What about *boisterous* and *orderly?*

George and Jennifer are brother and sister, but they are completely different. Jennifer is very shy and likes to be by herself a lot, but George is a real extrovert. Jennifer usually plays quietly without making any trouble for anyone, while George is almost always boisterous. Jennifer is also very orderly. On the other hand, George throws his clothes and toys all over his room so it looks as though a hurricane hit it.

Words like *but, while, on the other hand, although,* and *however* tell you that two things are different—opposites. When you see that Jennifer is shy and likes to be by herself, BUT George is an extrovert, you know that an extrovert is a person who is not shy and who likes to be with other people. If you follow the same logic, you can guess that *boisterous* means "loud" (the opposite of *quiet*) and that *orderly* means "neat and tidy."

FOR YOUR INFORMATION

It isn't always possible to figure out what a word means from context. But even if you have to look the word up in a dictionary, the context is important. Sometimes words have more than one meaning. So when you look them up, you still need the context to know which meaning is the one you want. Imagine you were reading this paragraph, and you didn't know what the word *plane* meant.

Grace decided the time had come to fix the drawer. She hadn't been able to close it for a week. She started to look for a plane, but after twenty minutes of looking, she gave up. She had everything except the one thing she needed to fix that drawer.

You look up *plane* in the dictionary, and this is what you find:

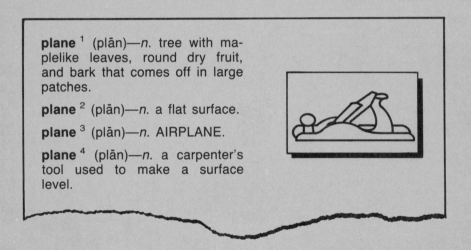

plane [1] (plān)—*n.* tree with maplelike leaves, round dry fruit, and bark that comes off in large patches.

plane [2] (plān)—*n.* a flat surface.

plane [3] (plān)—*n.* AIRPLANE.

plane [4] (plān)—*n.* a carpenter's tool used to make a surface level.

Which of these meanings fits into the paragraph you were reading? Obviously, the woman doesn't need a tree, a flat surface, or an airplane to fix her drawer. She needs a tool, so the meaning after plane [4] is the one that works in this context.

Self-Test

Answer the questions. Then compare your answers with those in *Answers and Explanations* on page 44.

Questions 1–2 are based on the following paragraph.

The largest part of the human brain is the cerebrum. It is the front part of the brain behind the forehead. Its major function is thinking. It controls memory, feelings, senses, and personality. The cerebellum, the part of the brain that is located behind the cerebrum, is involved in muscle movement and balance. The brain stem is located at the base of the skull. It controls all the automatic functions of the body like the heartbeat, breathing, swallowing, and digestion. It is the most primitive part of the brain.

Put an X next to the best answer.

1. The cerebellum is
   _____ (1) the part of the brain that is different from the cerebrum and the brain stem.
   _____ (2) the same part of the brain as the brain stem.
   _____ (3) a certain kind of personality.
   _____ (4) the same part of the brain as the cerebrum.
   _____ (5) a feeling or an idea.

2. Automatic functions of the body are
   _____ (1) body activities that you can control.
   _____ (2) thinking and feeling.
   _____ (3) anything to do with the personality.
   _____ (4) any activity that involves muscle movement.
   _____ (5) body activities that you usually can't control.

Questions 3–7 are based on the following instructions.

In the instructions, there are arrows pointing to certain objects. Read the instructions. Then fill in the blanks using these words:

plastic anchor	hole
surface of wall	fixture
screw	

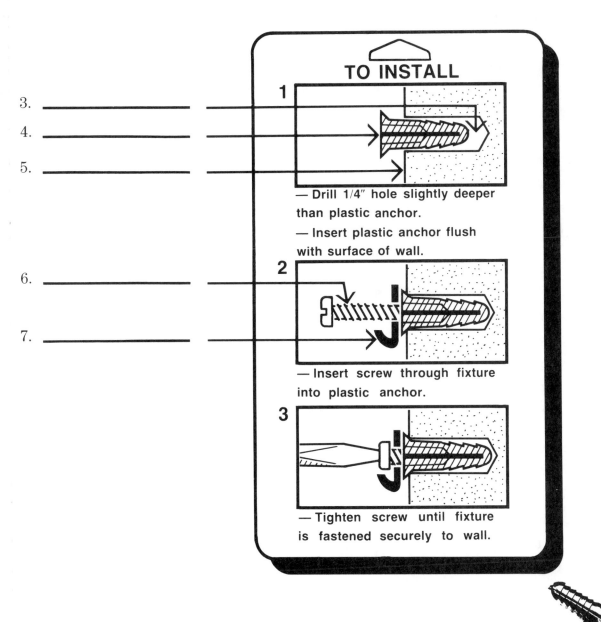

3. _____

4. _____

5. _____

6. _____

7. _____

TO INSTALL

1
— Drill 1/4" hole slightly deeper than plastic anchor.
— Insert plastic anchor flush with surface of wall.

2
— Insert screw through fixture into plastic anchor.

3
— Tighten screw until fixture is fastened securely to wall.

The Mississippi River is a great builder of land. During floods, it leaves rich deposits of mud and sand along its lower shores. These deposits create fertile farm land. In addition, the Mississippi River deposits sediment in the Gulf of Mexico year after year. It has formed a delta, a land deposit at the mouth of the river. This land deposit is shaped much like a triangle. It was named *delta* after the fourth letter of the Greek alphabet, which is also shaped like a triangle.

Put an X next to the best answer.

8. The word "deposit" in the second and third sentences means
   _____ (1) money you put in a bank.
   _____ (2) part of a river.
   _____ (3) mud and sand that the river carries and then leaves in different places along the river.
   _____ (4) a mixture of water, mud, and sand used as building material.
   _____ (5) a kind of farm.

9. "Fertile" in the third sentence probably means
   _____ (1) good for making building material.
   _____ (2) carried away by floods.
   _____ (3) near the Mississippi River.
   _____ (4) good for making pottery.
   _____ (5) good for growing things.

10. "Delta" in sentence 5 means
   _____ (1) the fourth letter of the Greek alphabet.
   _____ (2) a land deposit at the mouth of a river.
   _____ (3) an area of land along the shores of a river.
   _____ (4) good farm land.
   _____ (5) none of the above.

11. Look at the definitions from the dictionary. What is the meaning of *deposit* in this sentence?

The Mississippi deposits sediment in the Gulf of Mexico.

deposit (di päz´it)—*vt.* 1. to put money in the bank. 2. to put down or leave, as a river leaves sediment along its shores.—*n.* 1. something placed somewhere for safekeeping. 2. something that is laid down or left lying somewhere, like mud and dirt after a flood.

Deposit means _____

_____

THINKING AND WRITING

1. Read the following sentences. Then complete the answer.

John Stanley was the most belligerent person I have ever met. Luckily for him, however, his wife was very good-natured and refused to fight.

A belligerent person is someone who_____

_____

_____

2. Read the following sentences. Then complete the answer.

Whenever you go to a job interview, you should take your resume with you. In your resume, be sure to include information about your education, your work experience, and any special abilities that you have.

A resume would tell an employer_____

_____

_____

Compare your answers with those in *Answers and Explanations* on page 46.

STRATEGIES FOR SUCCESS

GETTING MEANING FROM CONTEXT

You can usually find clues to a word's meaning within the sentence or passage itself.

STRATEGY 1: Think it through.

1. Think about the context. That is, think about what the whole sentence or paragraph is about.
2. Use your logic to figure out what the word might mean.

Example: What does *victim* mean in this paragraph?

> ### ROBBERY AT KNIFE POINT
> Two people were robbed at knife point outside the Palace Hotel last night. The victims lost over $1,000, but were unharmed. They were able to give the police a fairly good description of the robber. They said the culprit was short, about 5′4″, with long, curly blond hair and a beard.

There was a robbery, and the victims were part of it. They lost $1,000. So *victim* means "the people who were robbed."

Write: Read the paragraph again. What does *culprit* mean? Use Strategy 1.

_____

_____

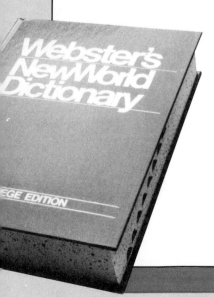

STRATEGY 2: Look for punctuation marks and special words.

1. Look for a comma (,) a dash (–), or a colon (:). A definition of the word might follow.
2. Look for words like *such as*, *like*, and *for example*. One or more examples of the word might follow.

Example: Read the following sentence. What does *maladies* mean?

> Pete Jackson is studying to be an otolaryngologist, a doctor who treats maladies of the ears, nose, and throat such as sore throats, earaches, and colds.

After the words *such as*, you see some examples of maladies—sore throats, earaches, and colds. What do all these have in common? They are illnesses. Maladies must be illnesses.
Write: Read the sentence again. What is an otolaryngologist? Use Strategy 2.

_____

_____

STRATEGY 3: Try to figure out what a word DOESN'T mean.

1. Use your logic to figure out what the word means.
2. Look for words like *but, while, on the other hand, although,* and *however*.

Example: Read the sentence below. What does *minuscule* mean?

> All the houses in the neighborhood were huge mansions, but there was one minuscule house at the end of the street.

The word *but* tells you that one house is not huge. The opposite of *huge* is *small*, so *minuscule* probably means "small."
Write: Read the following paragraph. What does *benign* mean? Use Strategy 3.

When we hear the word *tumor*, we always think of the dangerous kind, the kind that grows rapidly and can kill a person. However, many tumors are benign.

_____

_____

Compare your answers with those in *Answers and Explanations* on page 46.

Answers and Explanations

1. (1) You are told that the cerebellum is part of the brain, so (3) and (5) are wrong. Since it is behind the cerebrum, you can guess that it is not part of the cerebrum. Since it has different functions from the brain stem, you can guess that it is not part of the brain stem.

2. (5) After the words "automatic functions of the body," you see the word "like" and then several other words. You can imagine, because of the word *like*, that these words are examples of automatic functions of the body. All of them describe activities that we do not normally control or even think about. So, from these examples, you can guess that automatic functions of the body are activities that you usually can't control.

3. – 7.

3. hole

4. plastic anchor

5. surface of wall

6. screw

7. fixture

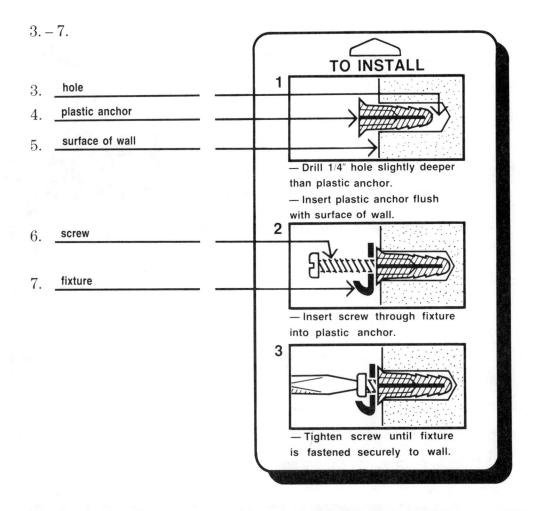

TO INSTALL

1
— Drill 1/4" hole slightly deeper than plastic anchor.
— Insert plastic anchor flush with surface of wall.

2
— Insert screw through fixture into plastic anchor.

3
— Tighten screw until fixture is fastened securely to wall.

The instructions say to drill a hole and insert the plastic anchor. There is only one thing in the picture that is in or inserted into another thing. So you know that the hole is the empty space (3.), and the plastic anchor is the thing inserted into the space (4.). Since the hole is drilled in the wall, you can guess that the third arrow is pointing to the surface of the wall (5.).

The instructions say to insert the screw into the plastic anchor, so the thing going into the anchor is the screw (6.). The screw should go through the fixture. In the picture, the screw goes through the black line, which might be a hook or a picture. The black line has to be the fixture (7.).

8. (3) The paragraph says the river "leaves rich deposits of mud and sand along its lower shores." So you know that deposits are mud and sand and that they are left somewhere. Even if you don't know that *shore* means the side of the river, you know the answer has to be (3). It is the only answer that tells about something being left somewhere.

9. (5) The paragraph says that "these deposits create fertile farm land." Land that is good for farming is good for growing things.

10. (2) In the fifth sentence, you see the word "delta." It is followed by a comma and a definition.

11. *Deposit* means "to put down or leave, as a river leaves sediment along its shores."

THINKING AND WRITING

1.   A belligerent person is someone who is not good-natured and who will fight.

    The word *however* tells you that John's wife is not belligerent. So you know that John is the opposite of a person who is good-natured and who refuses to fight.

2.   A resume would tell an employer about your education, your work experience, and any special abilities that you have.

    The second sentence says what is included in a resume.

STRATEGIES FOR SUCCESS

Strategy 1

    Culprit means "robber" in this paragraph.

Strategy 2

    An otolaryngologist is a doctor who treats illnesses of the ears, nose, and throat.

Strategy 3

    Benign means it isn't dangerous or it doesn't kill.

THE MAIN IDEA

WRITERS want to make things clear to the reader. To do this, they organize their ideas in a way that makes them easy to understand. Usually they group ideas about the same topic, or subject, into a paragraph. Each paragraph will have one main idea and then several ideas or details that tell you more about the main idea. If you can pick out the main idea and the supporting ideas, it is easier for you to understand and remember the information.

1. THE TOPIC SENTENCE

MOST **written material** like books, textbooks, magazine articles, and newspaper stories are made up of one or more paragraphs. A paragraph is a group of sentences that follow one another on a page. The sentences are about the same idea. One paragraph is always separated from another. This is usually done by **indenting** the first sentence of each paragraph or, sometimes, by skipping a line. Count the paragraphs in this article.

WRITTEN MATERIAL. Anything that is written down.

INDENT. To start writing a few spaces in on a line.

> For years, when there was an automobile accident, the insurance company of the person who caused the accident had to pay all the bills. The other insurance company paid nothing. Therefore, it was very important to find out who caused an accident.
>
> Now many states have no-fault automobile insurance. This means that it doesn't matter who causes an accident. Each person's insurance company pays his or her own bills. With no-fault insurance, it is not necessary to know who caused the accident.
>
> But even after receiving money from their insurance company, it is still possible for the victims to sue the driver of the other car. The victims can do this if they have a serious personal injury, like a serious broken bone.

You can find the three paragraphs in this article because the first sentence of each paragraph is indented.

It is very helpful when written material is divided into paragraphs. When you see a new paragraph, you know that the writer

  1) is going to give you additional, but different, information about the preceding subject, or
  2) is changing the subject completely.

Read the article on page 48. Notice how each paragraph has a different **topic,** or main idea. The first paragraph tells you about automobile insurance years ago. The second explains no-fault insurance. The third tells when one driver can sue the other.

Just any group of sentences does not make a paragraph. In a paragraph, all the sentences must be about the same idea. Which of the following groups of sentences is a paragraph?

> People need help retraining for jobs. New jobs are being created every day. But they require new skills. To get these skills, people often have to go back to school. But many people have neither the money nor the time to do this. The government should set up a job-training program that pays people to go to school. When they finish their job training, the government should help these people find jobs.

> A rainbow is made up of seven colors: red, orange, yellow, green, blue, indigo, and violet. A pink room makes people calm; a red one makes them excited. Many animals can't see color. For example, dogs don't see colors nearly as clearly as humans.

The first group of sentences is a paragraph. All the sentences talk about jobs. But even more important, they are all about one main idea—retraining people for jobs. There are a lot of things you can say about jobs, but this group of sentences is a paragraph because the subject is **limited**—it talks only about retraining.

In the second group of sentences, every sentence is about color. All the sentences talk about the same THING—color. But they are not about the same IDEA. One sentence is about color in a rainbow. Another sentence is about how people feel about color. And two sentences are about how animals see color.

There is usually one sentence in a paragraph that tells you what the main idea is. Often it is the first sentence. In Unit 1, you practiced predicting what an article or a paragraph was about by reading the first sentence. You were able to do this because the main idea was usually given there.

Look at this example.

At one time, Daniel J. Travanti, Captain Furillo of TV's *Hill Street Blues*, had a drinking problem. When he came to New York to be an actor, he had problems finding a job, and he began to drink. Before long, he was a serious alcoholic. Now, like the character he plays on TV, he has stopped drinking completely.

The sentence that gives the main idea (the first sentence in this paragraph) is called the **topic sentence**. The other sentences give you more information, or more **details**, about the main idea. In a good paragraph, all the sentences are related to the main idea.

Sometimes the topic sentence isn't at the beginning of a paragraph. It can be in the middle, or at the end, or anywhere in between. If it's in the middle, that's usually because the writer wants to have a short **introduction** to the paragraph. The introduction is put there to get you interested. It starts you thinking about things you know. This will help you understand the main idea of the paragraph.

In the following paragraph, which sentence is the topic sentence? How many sentences make up the introduction to the paragraph?

> **Some people say it's boring. Others say it's only for grandmothers. Others think it's a waste of time. But many people find needlepoint interesting and relaxing. Six-foot-five, 280-pound Rosey (Roosevelt) Grier, who used to play football for both the New York Giants and the Los Angeles Rams, does needlepoint as a hobby. He says it helps him relax and stay calm. He takes his needlepoint with him to card games and works on it to help himself keep a poker face. As you can imagine, no one ever calls him a sissy.**

The first sentence talks about something that is boring. But is the paragraph about something boring? No. If you read further, you will see that most of the paragraph talks about how interesting and relaxing needlepoint is. None of the first three sentences gives you this main idea. These sentences are just an introduction to get you interested. You have to read to the fourth sentence to find the main idea.

Sometimes the topic sentence is near the end of a paragraph. It may even be the last sentence. Writers put it there when they want to build up to the main idea. First, you get information or details about the main idea. Then, the writer tells you the main idea. Read this paragraph.

It was 4:30 in the morning on April 12, 1861. Suddenly, there was a flash of light. A mortar shell burst over Fort Sumter in Charleston, South Carolina. For 34 hours, the Confederate troops from the South battered the Federal troops who were in the fort. Finally, Major Robert Anderson, the Federal commander of the fort, agreed to surrender the fort to the Confederates. The next day, President Abraham Lincoln asked the northern states for 75,000 fighting men. The American Civil War had begun.

As you read this paragraph, you realize that each sentence gives you information about something that happened. Some of the sentences tell about firing on a fort. One is about surrendering the fort. And one is about President Lincoln. Why are all of these sentences in one paragraph? How are they related? When you read the last sentence, you know. All of these sentences tell about the beginning of the Civil War. The last sentence is the topic sentence, because all the other sentences in the paragraph relate to it.

*F*OR YOUR INFORMATION

Newspaper reporters use paragraphs differently from most other writers. Sometimes a paragraph is only one long sentence.

HEARNS K.O.'S SHULER IN 1!

Thomas Hearns, the 27-year-old fighter from Detroit, won the North American Boxing Federation's middleweight title when he knocked out James Shuler, the champion, in the first round.

One minute and 13 seconds into the match, Hearns hit Shuler with a right hand that put the loser on his back on the canvas.

When the referee, Richard Steele, finished his 10-count, Hearns threw his hands up in the sign of victory and left the ring grinning.

Hearns made $1 million for the fight with Shuler tonight. If he gets a rematch with Hagler, who beat him in three rounds last April, he'll earn $3.5 million.

Notice that the main idea of the article and the most important information are in the first sentence. All the sentences or paragraphs that follow just fill in the details. This is true of almost all news stories. Reporters do this for a reason: if you are in a hurry, you can just read the first part of an article and get almost all the information you need.

1. Put an X next to the group of sentences that is a paragraph.

   ____ (1) Try to avoid injury whenever possible. Statistics show that most people are injured in their own homes. Don't put butter on burns. Don't move a person who is seriously injured. For example, once I was injured and had to wait two hours before anyone heard me yell.

   ____ (2) There are several things you should do if you see a person who is seriously injured. First, move the person as little as possible. Find out if the person is breathing. Then cover the person, and if the person is on his or her back, raise the person's feet. Try to control bleeding if there is any, and get medical help as soon as possible.

2. Write the topic sentence of the paragraph you chose in question 1.

   _____

   _____

   _____

Find the topic sentence in each of the following paragraphs. Write the topic sentence in the space after the paragraph.

3. The date was February 20, 1962. The place was Cape Canaveral, Florida. John Glenn was strapped into his seat. Glenn was about to travel around the earth in space. It was something no American had done before. He began to count: Ten, nine, eight, seven, six, five, four, three, two, one, blast off. Huge flames shot out of the rocket, and the spacecraft began to rise.

   _____

   _____

   _____

4.   Making a circle with the thumb and first finger is considered a friendly gesture in the United States. It means "Great" or "OK." In France, it means "You're worth zero." Nodding the head up and down usually means "Yes," but not in Turkey. There, it means "No!" Thumbs up in the U.S. means everything is all right. In northern Greece, it's an insult. It's the same as giving someone the finger! When you travel, think before you make a gesture because you never know what it might mean!

_____

_____

_____

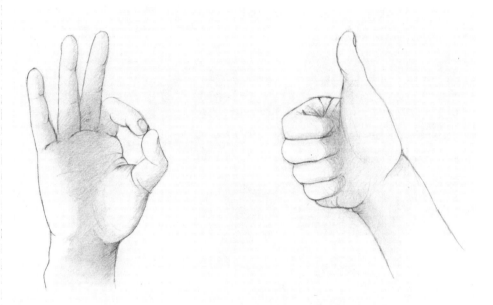

5.   It's exciting and sometimes dangerous. But men and women of all ages are doing it. The new sport called skydiving is becoming very popular. Skydiving is jumping out of an airplane with a parachute. It's not difficult. But you have to be pretty brave. First you jump out of the plane. Then you pull the rip cord on your parachute. This opens the chute. Then all you do is drift silently to the ground.

_____

_____

_____

2. THE UNSTATED MAIN IDEA

SOME paragraphs **state** their topic or main idea clearly in the first sentence. In other paragraphs, you have to look farther into the paragraph to find the topic sentence. And in many paragraphs, there is no topic sentence at all. You have to read all the sentences very carefully. Then you have to decide what one main idea all of them tell about. This is sometimes difficult. You have to come up with the main idea yourself. The writer doesn't do it for you. The writer just gives you the details or information about the topic. YOU have to figure out what the main idea is. Read the following paragraph.

STATE. To write or say something.

Since Peterson, a single parent, has to get the kids up and dressed and then take them to school, he gets to work late almost every morning. Whenever he meets friends after work, he looks at his watch constantly to see if it's time to get the kids. At 6:30 he picks them up from the day-care center and heads home to cook dinner. He gets the kids to bed by nine. After doing the dishes, he has a beer in front of the TV, or if he has the energy, he plays his banjo. He figures that he sees his girlfriend about two hours a week.

There isn't one sentence—a topic sentence—in the paragraph on page 56 that gives you the main idea. But all of the sentences are talking about one thing. Which of the following sentences do you think gives the main idea of the paragraph?

1. Peterson is a single parent.

2. Peterson spends a lot of time with his kids.

3. Peterson is so busy that he doesn't have much time for himself.

4. It's difficult for Peterson to work and take care of his kids.

5. Peterson doesn't get to spend much time with his girlfriend because he has to take care of his kids.

Number 1 is true. But the main idea is more than just the fact that Peterson is a single parent. Number 2, number 4, and number 5 are true too. But they only tell part of what the paragraph is about. Number 3 is the best choice. It includes all the ideas in the paragraph. Every sentence in the paragraph **demonstrates** that Peterson is so busy that he doesn't have much time for himself.

DEMONSTRATE. To show, prove, or make clear by using examples.

Self-Test

Answer the questions. Then compare your answers with those in *Answers and Explanations* on page 70.

Read each paragraph. Then put an X next to the topic sentence.

1.   You'll probably have difficulty sleeping and, perhaps, headaches and constipation. You'll also cough—even more than you did when you were smoking. That's because your lungs are trying to clear out years of built-up tar. You may feel a tingling or numbness in different parts of your body too, because your blood circulation is improving. Your heartbeat might also slow down, and your blood pressure will probably be lower.

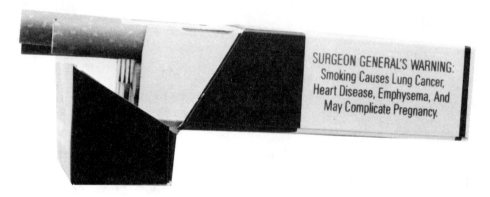

SURGEON GENERAL'S WARNING: Smoking Causes Lung Cancer, Heart Disease, Emphysema, And May Complicate Pregnancy.

_____ (1) You'll probably have difficulty sleeping and, perhaps, headaches and constipation.

_____ (2) You'll also cough—even more than you did when you were smoking.

_____ (3) Your heartbeat might also slow down, and your blood pressure will probably be lower.

_____ (4) That's because your lungs are trying to clear out years of built-up tar.

_____ (5) There is no topic sentence.

2.   Many laws have been passed, and many government agencies have been formed to protect consumers against

unfair business practices. If you feel that you have been cheated in any way, look in the phone book for the consumer-protection agency in your city. Call them, and they will tell you if there are any laws that can help you. Don't waste money on a lawyer until you have checked with your government agencies. They will probably be able to help you—for free!

_____ (1) Many laws have been passed, and many government agencies have been formed to protect consumers against unfair business practices.

_____ (2) They will probably be able to help you—for free!

_____ (3) Call them, and they will tell you if there are any laws that can help you.

_____ (4) Don't waste money on a lawyer until you have checked with your government agencies.

_____ (5) There is no topic sentence.

3.   When he was criticized for spending public money to pamper his dog, Fala, Franklin D. Roosevelt said, "I don't resent attacks, but Fala does resent them." The public loved him for it. Richard Nixon swore he would never give up his cocker spaniel, Checkers. Many think that helped him get the nomination for Vice-President. When Lyndon Johnson picked up his beagles, Him and Her, by the ears, he got hate mail.

_____ (1) The public loved him for it.

_____ (2) Richard Nixon swore he would never give up Checkers.

_____ (3) Many think that helped him get the nomination for Vice-President.

_____ (4) When Lyndon Johnson picked up his beagles by the ears, he got hate mail.

_____ (5) There is no topic sentence.

4.   A few days after reporting for football, George Gipp had established a few things about himself. Physically, at six feet and 180 pounds, wearing the sturdy canvas-and-moleskin football uniform of the time, he could run the 100-yard dash in 10.1 seconds, throw pinpoint passes half the length of the field, and boom off punts of 60 yards or more. Socially, he was a modest fellow with few close friends, easygoing to the point of indifference. Personally, he was totally untamed, a potential star to whom practice was a bore, discipline something to be ignored.

(Cox, James A. "Was 'the Gipper' really for real? You can bet he was." *Smithsonian*, December 1985, pp. 130–150.)

The real Gipper, George Gipp, in 1920 just before his death from pneumonia at 25.

Ronald Reagan, 6 feet and 180 pounds. In 1940, he starred as George Gipp in the film.

____ (1) A few days after reporting for football, George Gipp had established a few things about himself.

____ (2) He could run the 100-yard dash in 10.1 seconds, throw pinpoint passes half the length of the field, and boom off punts of 60 yards or more.

____ (3) Socially, he was a modest fellow with few close friends, easygoing to the point of indifference.

____ (4) Personally, he was totally untamed.

____ (5) There is no topic sentence.

Read each paragraph. **Then put an X next to the sentence that gives the main idea.**

5.   After gaining its independence from Mexico in 1836, Texas became an independent nation. It joined the United States in 1845. The entire Southwest was then added in 1848, as a result of the Mexican War. Still more land was acquired in 1867, when the United States bought Alaska from Russia. Then Hawaii, which had been a kingdom, became a U.S. territory in 1898.

    ____ (1) The history of Texas is very interesting.

    ____ (2) A lot of land that is now part of the U.S. once belonged to Mexico.

    ____ (3) The U.S. acquired land in a lot of different ways.

    ____ (4) Both Alaska and Hawaii were acquired after Texas.

    ____ (5) Texas was an independent country for nine years.

6.   In 1975, animals started acting strangely in and around the city of Haicheng, China. Earthquake experts noticed this, and they predicted an earthquake. Within three days, there was a huge quake that could have killed thousands.

    ____ (1) Experts have not found a way to predict earthquakes.

    ____ (2) Animals in China act differently from animals in other countries.

    ____ (3) It took three days to predict an earthquake in 1975.

    ____ (4) Experts predicted an earthquake because animals were acting strangely.

    ____ (5) There are many earthquakes in China.

3. SUPPORTING IDEAS

FINDING the main idea of a paragraph is very important. It keeps your mind on what the writer is trying to get across in the whole reading passage. But there is more to a paragraph than the main idea. Writers add sentences to explain, **prove**, or give you examples of exactly what they're talking about. These sentences give **supporting ideas** or details.

Read the following paragraph. Notice how the last seven sentences support the main idea in the first sentence.

PROVE. To show without any doubt that something is true.

SUPPORTING IDEA. A sentence that gives information about or proves the main idea.

Hawaii is a perfect vacation spot. First of all, it's beautiful. It sits in the middle of the clear, blue waters of the Pacific. And its white sandy beaches stretch for miles. Its waters are full of beautiful shells and tropical fish, so it's a paradise for scuba divers and snorkelers. If you like nightlife, there are plenty of clubs, restaurants, and discotheques. Finally, the variety of cultures on Hawaii makes it a fascinating place to visit. The people of Polynesia, China, Japan, and Europe create an exotic atmosphere unique to these islands.

The writer wants to prove to you that this island is a perfect place to go on a vacation. How does he do it? He describes all the things about the island that might make you want to visit it. There are basically four supporting ideas:

1. It's beautiful.
2. It's a paradise for divers and snorkelers.
3. There are plenty of things to do at night.
4. It's exotic—there are a lot of different cultures there.

The supporting ideas of a paragraph give you more information about the main idea. All the sentences above prove a point. But they also answer some questions about Hawaii. Where is Hawaii? Who lives there? What are some things you can do in Hawaii? What are the beaches like?

Now look at this paragraph.

There are a lot of different ways to cook vegetables. You can steam them, boil them, bake them, or fry them. You can also grill them over an open fire while you're cooking your hamburgers. Steamed, baked, and grilled vegetables keep more of their vitamins than boiled vegetables. Fried vegetables keep their vitamins too. But they are much more fattening when cooked that way.

The supporting ideas in this paragraph give you information. They tell you five ways to cook vegetables. (You can steam, boil, fry, grill, or bake them.) They also tell you the advantages and disadvantages of the different cooking methods. At the same time, the supporting ideas prove the main idea— that there are a lot of different ways to cook vegetables.

So supporting ideas have two purposes. One purpose is to explain or prove the main idea. The other is simply to give the reader information.

Self-Test

Answer the questions. Then compare your answers with those in *Answers and Explanations* on page 71.

Questions 1–3 are based on the following paragraph.

1. Read the paragraph and underline the topic sentence.

> **Putting an ad in the personal column of a newspaper can be an easy and safe way to meet interesting people. You just put in the ad and wait for the letters. After reading the letters, you decide who to call. You can meet the person for the first time in a coffee shop, park, or bar. This person never has to know where you live, your telephone number, or even your last name. You can check each other out and decide whether or not to see each other again—with no hard feelings.**

> Nice guy with good job, brown hair, hazel eyes, 6 ft tall on heavy side, age 32. My problem is I can't find the right girl. Maybe it's you.
>
> Box J3014

Put an X next to the best answer.

2. The supporting ideas in this paragraph tell you
   _____ (1) why personal ads are safe.
   _____ (2) why personal ads are easy.
   _____ (3) how to answer personal ads.
   _____ (4) both 1 and 2.
   _____ (5) both 2 and 3.

3. According to the paragraph, which of these is NOT a "safe" place to meet someone who answers your personal ad?
   _____ (1) A coffee shop
   _____ (2) A bar
   _____ (3) Your house or apartment
   _____ (4) A park
   _____ (5) All of the above

Questions 4–5 are based on the following paragraph.

Most divorced men feel that the courts discriminate against them because they are men. The most obvious example of this is that the woman almost always gets custody of the children after a divorce. Also, it's the men that have to pay child support, while women almost never pay anything. For a year after Jeff Howard divorced his wife, he had one child. His wife had the other child. During that time, he paid his wife $400 a month in child support. Now his wife has decided that she wants Jeff to have custody of both children. But the court says she doesn't have to pay anything to help support them.

4. According to the writer, who usually pays child support after two people are divorced?

   _____ (1) The man

   _____ (2) The woman

   _____ (3) The courts

   _____ (4) The child

   _____ (5) None of the above

5. According to the writer, the courts discriminate against men. What supporting ideas are given to prove that?

   _____ (1) Women almost always get custody of the children after a divorce.

   _____ (2) Men have to pay child support and women don't.

   _____ (3) Jeff's wife has now decided that she wants him to have custody of the children.

   _____ (4) Both 1 and 2.

   _____ (5) Both 2 and 3.

Questions 6–7 are based on the following paragraph.

String instruments have strings. They are played with a bow or with the fingers. They include the violin, the cello, the bass violin, the harp, the guitar, and the banjo. The woodwinds are instruments that originally were made of wood. The principal ones are the oboe, the clarinet, the flute, and the bassoon. Instruments like the trumpet, the trombone, and the French horn are called brass. Obviously, they are all made of brass. Finally, the percussion instruments are the ones that you hit. They include all kinds of drums, the triangle, the cymbals, and the tambourine. These are the four basic types of musical instruments.

6. What is the topic sentence?
   _____ (1) String instruments have strings.
   _____ (2) They include the violin, the cello, the bass violin, the harp, the guitar, and the banjo.
   _____ (3) Obviously, they are all made of brass.
   _____ (4) These are the four basic types of musical instruments.
   _____ (5) None of the above.

7. A tambourine is
   _____ (1) a string instrument.
   _____ (2) a woodwind.
   _____ (3) a brass instrument.
   _____ (4) a percussion instrument.
   _____ (5) none of the above.

THINKING AND WRITING

Use the sentences in this paragraph to fill in the chart below.

Small-claims court is set up to handle disagreements that involve less than $1,000. Small-claims court is cheap and easy to use. Suppose someone sells you a used washing machine, and tells you it's only five years old and it's in perfect condition. But when you get it home, it doesn't work. If the person refuses to give you your money back, you can go to small-claims court and sue him or her. All you have to have are the name and address of the person you want to sue, and proof that you have a good reason to sue. You take this information to the court offices, and they will give you a date to come to court. In most places, this costs under five dollars, and you don't need a lawyer.

Topic Sentence _____

_____

_____

Important Supporting Ideas

1. _____

_____

2. _____

_____

3. _____

_____

Compare your answers with those in *Answers and Explanations* on page 72.

1. THE TOPIC SENTENCE

A paragraph often has one sentence that states the main idea. This is the topic sentence.

STRATEGY: Find the sentence that gives the main idea.

1. Look for the sentence that ties all the other sentences together.
2. Remember that the topic sentence can be anywhere in the paragraph.

Example: What is the topic sentence of this paragraph?

Until recently, the quality of life in American cities was on the decline. People and businesses started moving to the suburbs. As they moved, cities lost tax money. Schools, housing, and important city services began to decline. Unemployment grew.

The last four sentences give *examples* of the decline of the quality of life in cities. They are supporting ideas. The first sentence ties the examples, or supporting ideas, together. It's the topic sentence.

Write: Write the topic sentence of the following paragraph.

We do exercises. We do aerobics. We lift weights. We eat whole grains and lots of fruit and vegetables. Getting and staying healthy has become the passion of the 80s.

_____

_____

2. THE UNSTATED MAIN IDEA

Sometimes there is no topic sentence in a paragraph. You have to figure out the main idea yourself.

STRATEGY: Think it through.

1. Ask yourself these questions:

a) What is each sentence (supporting idea) about?

b) How do all the sentences relate to each other?

2. Use your logic to figure out the main idea.

Example: What is the main idea of this paragraph?

One symptom of a heart attack is pain in your chest. Another is shortness of breath. Some people also have pain in an arm or in their neck.

Each of the sentences (supporting ideas) gives a symptom of a heart attack. So the main idea of the paragraph must be that heart attacks have several symptoms.

Write: Write the main idea of the following paragraph.

The first type of volcano, the active volcano, always shows signs of volcanic action. The second type, the dormant volcano, is a volcano that hasn't erupted in a long time, but it might someday. The third type, the extinct volcano, is one that hasn't erupted in hundreds of years. It is dead.

_____

_____

_____

Compare your answers with those in *Answers and Explanations* on page 72.

Answers and Explanations

1. THE TOPIC SENTENCE

1. (2) All these sentences talk about one main idea—what to do if a person is injured. All the sentences in the first group talk about injuries, but there is no main idea connecting all the sentences.

2. There are several things you should do if you see a person who is seriously injured.

   This sentence gives the main idea of the paragraph. All the other sentences in the paragraph relate to it and give more information about it.

3. Glenn was about to travel around the earth in space.

   All the other sentences in the paragraph give small details of an event or happening. One gives the time, one the place, etc. But this is the only sentence that tells what is happening.

4. When you travel, think before you make a gesture because you never know what it might mean!

   Every sentence in this paragraph except the topic sentence gives an example of a gesture and its different meanings. The last sentence is the topic sentence because it shows how all these examples are related—gestures mean different things in different places.

5. The new sport called skydiving is becoming very popular.

   The first two sentences are just an introduction. After the topic sentence, all the other sentences give more details about jumping out of an airplane.

2. THE UNSTATED MAIN IDEA

1. (5) The main idea of this paragraph is that people usually

have physical reactions when they quit smoking. Each sentence in the paragraph gives just one specific example of a reaction. All are too limited to be the topic sentence.

2. (1) All the other sentences in the paragraph give more details about this main idea.

3. (5) All the sentences in this paragraph give examples of an idea—people in the U.S. like people who treat their pets well. But that idea is not stated.

4. (1) Each sentence following the first gives examples of things Gipp had established about himself.

5. (3) The paragraph tells how several states became part of the U.S. Sentences 1, 2, 4, and 5 tell about only one state or part of the country. They are too limited.

6. (4) All the sentences in this paragraph are related to the idea that the actions of animals helped predict an earthquake.

3. SUPPORTING IDEAS

1.   The topic sentence is the first sentence. All the other sentences give more details about why putting an ad in the personal column can be an easy and safe way to meet someone.

2. (4) There is nothing in the paragraph about (3) how to answer a personal ad.

3. (3) All the other answers are suggested in the paragraph as safe places to meet someone.

4. (1) Look at the third sentence in the paragraph.

5. (4) Answer (3) is part of an example. It relates to the other

ideas in the example, but it doesn't give any information that proves that courts discriminate against men.

6. (4) This is the only sentence in the paragraph that ties all the other sentences together.

7. (4) The ninth sentence tells you that tambourines are included in the group of percussion instruments.

THINKING AND WRITING

Topic Sentence: Small-claims court is cheap and easy to use.
Important Supporting Ideas

1. All you have to have are the name and address of the person you want to sue, and proof that you have a good reason to sue.

2. You take this information to the court offices, and they will give you a date to come to court.

3. In most places, this costs under five dollars, and you don't need a lawyer.

    Sentences 1 and 2 above show how small-claims court is easy to use. Sentence 3 shows that it is cheap. All the other sentences in the paragraph, except the topic sentence, only give an example of when you might want to use the small-claims court.

STRATEGIES FOR SUCCESS

1. The Topic Sentence

Getting and staying healthy has become the passion of the 80s.

2. The Unstated Main Idea

There are three types of volcanoes.

ORGANIZATION OF A PARAGRAPH

ALMOST all paragraphs have a main idea and several supporting ideas. But these ideas are not always organized in the same way. When writing about history or telling a story, a writer might organize the supporting ideas in the order they happened. If a writer wants to prove something to you, he or she might organize the supporting ideas into an example.

By organizing the supporting ideas in a certain way, the main idea will become clearer. If you can recognize how a paragraph is organized, you will be able to understand more easily what the writer is telling you.

1. CHRONOLOGICAL ORDER

TO understand a paragraph, it's necessary to find the main idea. Then it's important to be able to pick out the important supporting ideas and details. It also helps if the reader can see how the ideas are **organized**—that is, how they fit together.

There are several different ways to organize a paragraph. One way is to put the details down **in sequence**—in the order they happened. This is called **chronological order**. The writer starts with what happened first. Then the writer tells what happened next, what happened after that, and so on.

Look at this example.

ORGANIZED. Put in a certain order.

IN SEQUENCE. In order— usually according to time.

CHRONOLOGICAL ORDER. The order of things by time—what happened first, second, next, etc.

Parícutin is a volcano in western Mexico that appeared out of nowhere and destroyed a town. One day in 1943, a farmer noticed that a small hill had grown in his cornfield. The next day the hill was bigger. A few days later, he saw that there was a crack in the hill. Then hot gas started coming out of the crack. Thirty minutes later, there was an explosion. A cloud of gas and ash shot into the air as high as four miles! The explosion continued, and soon the whole village was covered with lava and volcanic ash. Now a volcano 1,345 feet high stands where the cornfield and village used to be.

In the paragraph about the volcano, the first sentence is the topic sentence. Notice that after the topic sentence, all the sentences tell a story. The second sentence begins the story. It tells what happened first. All the others tell what happened next in time.

There are certain words in this paragraph that help you figure out how the paragraph is organized. These words are like clues. If you see one or two of them in a paragraph, you can guess that the ideas are organized chronologically. Read the paragraph again. Write down two or three words that you think show time order.

1. _____

2. _____

3. _____

Maybe you wrote *next, later, then, now,* or *soon.* A writer might also use words and **phrases** like *first, second, after that, before, yesterday,* and *later.* The date (January 10), a year (1988), or a time (10:00) could also be clues.

PHRASE. An expression of two or more words.

Stories are often organized in chronological order. Newspaper articles are a good example. Recipes and directions are usually organized in this way too.

Self-Test

Answer the questions. Then compare your answers with those in *Answers and Explanations* on page 92.

Put an X next to the best answer.

1. Which of the following paragraphs is organized chronologically?

    _____ (1) Today, almost eight out of every ten Americans live in a metropolitan area. Metropolitan areas are growing bigger and bigger, and we are told that one day the northeastern seacoast will be one big city. Some people say that this is because it's difficult to make a living on small farms. So farmers are selling out to big farm companies and moving to the cities to find work.

    _____ (2) In 1800, only one person out of ten in the United States lived in a city. By 1900, four people out of ten lived in cities. More and more people immigrated to the U.S., and most of them moved into the cities too. By 1916, almost half of the population lived in cities. Today, almost eight out of every ten Americans live in a metropolitan area.

2. The paragraph you chose in question 1 is in chronological order because it

    _____ (1) tells how many people lived in cities in 1900.

    _____ (2) contains several facts arranged by time.

    _____ (3) tells about life in U.S. cities.

    _____ (4) all of the above.

    _____ (5) none of the above.

2. COMPARISON AND CONTRAST

ANOTHER way to organize a paragraph is to **compare** two things. Sometimes the writer will organize the ideas and details in a paragraph to show how two things are alike or how two things are different. Sometimes the writer will do both in the same paragraph.

Look at this example.

> Snorkeling and scuba diving are alike in some ways and yet very different in others. Both are water sports, and for both you need fins and a mask. However, when you snorkel, you just float on the surface of the water and breathe air through your snorkel. When you scuba dive, you go under the water and stay there for twenty or thirty minutes. This means you need an oxygen tank and other expensive equipment. Also, because scuba diving can be dangerous, you have to take a special course and pass a test before you can dive. On the other hand, to snorkel you need almost no training, and there is very little danger.

 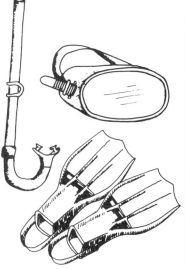

COMPARE. To show how things are alike or different.

When you read the topic sentence (the first sentence), the words *alike* and *different* tell you that this paragraph is probably going to compare two things—scuba diving and snorkeling.

First you find out how they are alike:

ALIKE

- water sports
- use fins and mask

Then you learn how they are different:

DIFFERENT

Scuba Diving	Snorkeling
• Need oxygen tank	• Breathe air
• Stay underwater 20-30 minutes	• Stay on surface
• Can be dangerous	• Not dangerous
• Need a special course and test	• Almost no training needed

The two charts above **summarize** the paragraph and show you in a short form how the paragraph is organized.

There are several words in the paragraph on page 77 that show that two things are being compared. Complete the following list.

alike	_____
different	_____
_____	_____

SUMMARIZE. To give only the most important ideas or details about something.

You probably wrote *both, also, however,* and *on the other hand. Both* and *also* indicate the writer is going to say how two things are alike. *On the other hand* and *however* show you that the writer is going to tell how two things are different. Some other clues that indicate comparison are *but, still, so, similar, too, like, unlike, more . . . than,* and *yet.*

Self-Test

Answer the questions. Then compare your answers with those in *Answers and Explanations* on page 92.

Questions 1–3 are based on the following paragraph.

Two of our most famous presidents had very similar lives. Abraham Lincoln was elected to the House of Representatives in 1847. Exactly 100 years later, John F. Kennedy was also elected to the House of Representatives. Both men became President of the United States 13 years after they were elected to Congress. Both men were assassinated, shot in the head, before they could finish their term in office. The day Lincoln was killed, his secretary, whose name was Kennedy, told him not to go to the theater. Kennedy's secretary, whose name was Lincoln, advised him not to go to Dallas. The man who killed Lincoln was killed before he could go on trial. So was the man who killed Kennedy. Both Lincoln and Kennedy were succeeded by a Vice-President named Johnson.

1. Write the topic sentence of this paragraph.

_____

_____

Put an X next to the best answer.

2. This paragraph tells

_____ (1) how the lives of presidents Kennedy and Lincoln were similar.

_____ (2) how the lives of presidents Kennedy and Lincoln were different.

_____ (3) only about President Kennedy.

_____ (4) only about President Lincoln.

_____ (5) none of the above.

3. The paragraph above is organized to show a comparison. Circle the words in the paragraph that show this type of organization.

Questions 4–6 are based on the following paragraph.

Recent research shows that men are more likely to be thin than women. First, men usually exercise more than women, and this helps them stay thin. Then, most men's bodies burn calories faster than most women's bodies do. Even more important, women's bodies just naturally have a higher fat content than men's. Women have more fat cells, and they store more fat. A man's body is normally only about 15–20% fat, while a woman's is 20–28%.

4. Underline the sentence in the paragraph that gives you the FIRST clue that two things are being compared.

Put an X next to the best answer.

5. In the sentence you underlined, what word or phrase shows that two things are being compared?

_____ (1) First

_____ (2) Then

_____ (3) More . . . than

_____ (4) Even more important . . .

_____ (5) Most

6. What two things are being compared?

_____ (1) Men's and women's bodies

_____ (2) Two different kinds of exercise

_____ (3) Men's and women's feelings about being fat

_____ (4) Two ways that the body burns calories

_____ (5) All of the above

3. CAUSE AND EFFECT

ANOTHER way to organize a paragraph is to show that one thing happened BECAUSE another thing happened. In other words, the first thing CAUSED the second thing to happen.

> During an earthquake, the earth shifts and moves. This causes shock waves to travel in all directions. The waves make the earth vibrate, and that makes buildings shake and fall. Sometimes a large crack opens up in the earth. If the earthquake starts under the sea, it may cause a huge wave that crashes onto the land and causes even more destruction.

First there is an earthquake. Then other things happen:
- Shock waves travel in all directions.
- The earth vibrates, buildings shake and fall.
- Sometimes a large crack opens up in the earth.
- A huge wave may crash onto the land.

These are the **effects**, or results, of the earthquake. The details in this paragraph are organized to show the reader that one thing caused several other things to happen. Some of the key words that point out cause and effect are *cause, effect, result, because, make, as a result, therefore, reason, so,* and *consequently.*

EFFECT. A result.

There is also another word that shows both cause and effect. Look at this paragraph.

> They had to decide soon, but it was hard. If they went on strike, they could all lose their jobs. But if they didn't, they would have to give up all hope of starting a union.

The *if* part of the sentence shows the cause. The other part of the sentence shows the effect. The key word is *if.*

Questions 1–2 are based on the following paragraph.

Did you know that owning a pet could help you live longer? High blood pressure and stress are two of the major causes of heart attacks. Some psychiatrists believe that having a pet may help people lower their blood pressure and reduce feelings of stress. Research has shown that if people pet and speak to animals, their blood pressure drops. Watching a fish tank can have the same results. Pets seem to help people relax and forget about themselves. As a result, stress is reduced, and along with it, the risk of having a heart attack.

Put an X next to the best answer.

1. According to the paragraph, owning a pet can
   _____ (1) lower blood pressure.
   _____ (2) reduce feelings of stress.
   _____ (3) reduce the risk of having a heart attack.
   _____ (4) help you relax.
   _____ (5) all of the above.

2. Which of these words show you that this paragraph is organized to show cause and effect?
   _____ (1) If
   _____ (2) Results
   _____ (3) As a result
   _____ (4) All of the above
   _____ (5) None of the above

Questions 3–4 are based on the following paragraph.

Everyone should have an aloe plant in the kitchen. This strange-looking plant can work miracles on burns. If you burn yourself cooking, just break one of the stems in the middle. You'll see a greenish jellylike substance. If you rub that substance over the burned area, the pain will stop almost immediately. Even better, the burn will not blister. Many people say that aloe makes a burn heal much faster.

3. What is the main idea of this paragraph?
   _____ (1) There is a greenish jellylike substance inside an aloe plant.
   _____ (2) The aloe plant can work miracles on burns.
   _____ (3) If you cook, you might burn yourself.
   _____ (4) The stems of the aloe plant break easily.
   _____ (5) Aloe prevents burns from blistering.

4. "Rub the jellylike substance from the aloe plant over a burn" is the cause. What is the effect?
   _____ (1) Break the stem of your aloe plant.
   _____ (2) The burn will disappear immediately.
   _____ (3) The pain will stop, and the burn won't blister.
   _____ (4) All of the above.
   _____ (5) None of the above.

4. EXAMPLES

Sometimes the writer gives an example to prove or **illustrate** the main idea. In this type of organization, all of the supporting sentences are related because they are part of an example. Look at the following paragraph. What is the topic sentence? What is the example?

> **Some home remedies tell you to do the exact opposite of what you should do. For example, people say it's good to put butter on a burn. Any doctor, however, will tell you that you should never put grease on a burn. The best thing to do is simply run cold water over the burned area.**

The first sentence is the topic sentence. The three sentences that follow relate to each other and to the topic sentence. They give an example of the main idea. Here is another example.

> Recently, Jane Brody applied for a management position in her company. She had been a secretary with the company for over ten years, and had often run her office when her boss was away. She had a college degree and had taken a six-month course in management. A man who had been with the company for only three years was given the job. He had no experience in management and had never taken any courses in that subject. When Brody protested, she was fired. She sued the company for sexual discrimination and won. Although sexual discrimination is hard to prove, many women have taken sexual discrimination cases to court and won.

The last sentence in the paragraph states the main idea. All the other sentences in the paragraph tell a story about Jane Brody. They are organized into an example that helps prove the main idea.

Words like *for example, an example of this is,* and *suppose* can help you recognize this type of organization.

*F*OR YOUR INFORMATION

In some paragraphs, the supporting ideas are organized in more than one way. Some of the ideas and details may be in chronological order, and others may be organized to show cause and effect or to give an example.

When you get a sprain, there are certain things you can do. The area is usually very painful, and it swells quickly. You should first wrap the area tightly and then put ice on it. Next, elevate it and rest it. Wrapping the area tightly keeps the swelling down, and the ice shrinks the blood vessels. You elevate the area so all fluids will drain out. You rest it so you won't hurt it again.

The first sentence is the topic sentence. The third and fourth sentences tell you in chronological order what you should do. Then the last two sentences are organized to show cause and effect. They tell what will happen if you wrap a sprain, put ice on it, elevate it, and rest it.

Questions 1–2 are based on the following paragraph.

According to Dennis McCarthy in his book, *Private Lives of the Presidents—What the Public Never Sees*, the secret-service agents who worked for Henry Kissinger said that he treated them like servants. But sometimes they got even by playing jokes on Kissinger. One day Mr. Kissinger asked an agent what he would do if they were attacked by terrorists. The agent thought for a minute and then said, "Well, sir, this gun carries six bullets, so I would probably be able to kill five of the terrorists. But my orders also say that *you* are not to be taken alive." Kissinger looked shocked for a few seconds and then said, "You're kidding, of course."

Put an X next to the best answer.

1. The example was put in this paragraph to prove that
   _____ (1) secret-service agents worked for Kissinger.
   _____ (2) Kissinger had a secret life.
   _____ (3) there were sometimes terrorist attacks on Kissinger.
   _____ (4) the secret-service agents sometimes got even by playing jokes on Kissinger.
   _____ (5) none of the above.

2. What word or phrase shows you that some of the supporting ideas in this paragraph are organized into an example?
   _____ (1) But
   _____ (2) So
   _____ (3) Of course
   _____ (4) And then
   _____ (5) None of the above

Questions 3–4 are based on the following paragraph.

Weather and climate are different. Weather is the general

condition of the atmosphere at one specific time and place. It changes every day. One day it can be hot and humid. The next morning it can rain. In the afternoon the sun can come out, and it can be cool and clear. Climate, on the other hand, is the average weather conditions of a place over a long period of time. Climate doesn't change. For example, we know that if we go to New York in the winter, it will probably be cold. But if we go to Florida, it will be much warmer.

3. The information in this paragraph is organized
_____ (1) in chronological order.
_____ (2) to show cause and effect.
_____ (3) to show a comparison.
_____ (4) to give one or more examples of the main idea.
_____ (5) both 3 and 4.

4. What words or expressions helped you answer question 3?
_____ (1) Different
_____ (2) For example
_____ (3) On the other hand
_____ (4) All of the above
_____ (5) None of the above

Question 5 is based on the following paragraph.

The population of the world is growing very fast, some people say too fast. Between the year 1 and the year 1650, the population doubled from 250 million to 500 million. That is, it took 1,650 years for the population to double. From 1650 to 1830, the population doubled again—in less than 200 years. Only 100 years later, in 1930, there were 2 billion people on earth, and just 40 years later, 4 billion! Now it is estimated that by the year 2000, there will be 8 billion people on earth.

5. The information in this paragraph is organized

_____ (1) in chronological order.

_____ (2) to show cause and effect.

_____ (3) to show a comparison.

_____ (4) both 1 and 2.

_____ (5) both 2 and 3.

Question 6 is based on the following paragraph.

The ancient Egyptians believed very strongly in life after death. Because of this, they carefully preserved dead bodies and buried them with clothes, furniture, food, and anything else they might need in the next life. To them, the graves of the dead were sacred. So they put a curse on anyone who opened one. Some people think the curses were effective. For example, in 1923, a group of archaeologists opened the tomb of the Egyptian king Tutankhamen. Before long, several of the people who had opened the tomb got a strange fever and died. Later, several visitors to the tomb got the same unexplained fever and died. To this day, some people believe that these people died because they dared to open a sacred tomb.

6. The information in this paragraph is organized in two ways. What are they?

_____ (1) In chronological order and to show cause and effect

_____ (2) To show cause and effect and to give an example to help prove an idea

_____ (3) To show a comparison and to show cause and effect

_____ (4) In chronological order and to give an example to help prove an idea

_____ (5) None of the above

THINKING AND WRITING

Read the paragraph and answer the questions.

The Homestead Act changed the face of the West forever. This law, passed in 1862, gave 160 acres of land to anyone who agreed to work the land for five years. Because of this law, people began settling in Nebraska, the Dakotas, and the plains of Kansas. A more negative effect of the law was to push the native Americans off their lands. The settlers wanted the land, and the government gave it to them. By the 1880s, most Indians were forced to live on reservations—on land so poor that no one else wanted it.

1. Write the topic sentence of the paragraph.

_____

2. This paragraph is organized in two ways. What are they?

_____

3. Write five words or phrases that helped you recognize this.

_____   _____   _____

_____   _____

4. What were two effects of the Homestead Act?

_____

_____

5. "Act" in this paragraph means the same as
   _____ (1) law.
   _____ (2) settler.
   _____ (3) acre.
   _____ (4) agreement.
   _____ (5) change.

Compare your answers with those in *Answers and Explanations* on page 93.

STRATEGIES FOR SUCCESS

ORGANIZATION OF A PARAGRAPH

The supporting ideas in a paragraph can be organized in several different ways: in chronological order, to show a comparison, to show cause and effect, or to form an example.

STRATEGY: Look for key words and phrases.

1. Look for words and phrases in the supporting ideas that might tell you how a paragraph is organized.
2. Check to see if the other supporting ideas are organized similarly.

Example 1: This paragraph is organized in two ways. What is the word in the first sentence that indicates one type of organization? What are the other words in the paragraph that point to this type of organization?

All hamburgers are not alike. They don't look the same, and they certainly don't taste the same. But did you know that nutritionally they are very different too? For example, a recent survey showed that a Burger King Whopper has 670 calories and gives you 40% of the protein you need in a day. On the other hand, a McDonald's Big Mac has only 563 calories. But it gives you 60% of your daily protein!

In the first sentence, the word *alike* shows that this paragraph is going to compare things. The other words that point to a comparison are *same, different,* and *on the other hand.*

Write: Some of the ideas in the paragraph above are organized in another way.   What is it? _____
Write the sentence that tells you this.

_____

_____

Example 2: How are the ideas organized in this paragraph?

> If a person stays out in the sun too long, he or she could get sunstroke. Get the person out of the sun and into a cool place. Put cool cloths or ice on the victim's skin to bring down the body temperature. Get medical help.

The supporting ideas in this paragraph tell you what to do for a victim of sunstroke. They are instructions. The instructions are organized in chronological order.

Write: It's usually easier to recognize chronological order when there are key words or expressions. Rewrite the paragraph above using these time expressions: *first, then, as soon as possible.*

_____

_____

_____

_____

_____

_____

_____

_____

_____

_____

Compare your answers with those in *Answers and Explanations* on page 94.

Answers and Explanations

1. CHRONOLOGICAL ORDER

1. (2) The facts in this paragraph are given in the order in which they happened. In the first paragraph, the facts explain WHY people moved to the city.

2. (2) is the correct answer. There are two time expressions in the first paragraph too: *today* and *one day*. But the facts are not in chronological order.

2. COMPARISON AND CONTRAST

1. Two of our most famous presidents had very similar lives.

   All the other sentences in the paragraph give more details about this main idea.

2. (1) All the information in the paragraph shows how the presidents' lives were similar.

3. similar, also, both, so

   All of these words indicate a comparison, usually one showing how things are alike.

4. In the first sentence, the words *more likely . . . than* tell you right away that there is going to be a comparison.

5. (3) The other words don't indicate a comparison.

6. (1) The whole paragraph is about men's and women's bodies.

3. CAUSE AND EFFECT

1. (5) All four answers give a result of owning a pet.

2. (4) All three of these words indicate organization to show cause and effect.

3. (2) All the sentences in this paragraph, except the first two, show that the aloe plant makes a burn stop hurting and helps it heal.

4. (3) Look at the fifth and sixth sentences in the paragraph.

4. EXAMPLES

1. (4) The whole example tells about a joke an agent played on Kissinger.

2. (5) There is no word or phrase in this paragraph that tells you for sure that an example follows. However, it's fairly clear that all the sentences in the second half of the paragraph are organized to tell a story about Kissinger.

3. (5) The first sentence compares weather and climate. All the other sentences in the paragraph talk about how they are different. Sentences 4, 5, and 6 give an example of how weather changes. The last two sentences give an example of how climate doesn't change.

4. (4) *Different* and *on the other hand* are used when talking about things or ideas that are not alike. Here they help you understand that this paragraph is organized to show a comparison. *For example* gives you a clue that some of the ideas are organized to give an example of the main idea.

5. (1) All the facts in this paragraph are listed in chronological order. The time expressions (dates) help you see this.

6. (2) The sentences in the first part of the paragraph are organized to show cause and effect. Words like *because of this* and *so* show you this. The last part of the paragraph is an example. The phrase *for example* helps you figure this out.

THINKING AND WRITING

1. The Homestead Act changed the face of the West forever.

   The second sentence explains what the Homestead Act was, and all the rest of the sentences show how the West changed because of the Act.

2. The paragraph is organized in chronological order and to show cause and effect.

Almost all the supporting ideas show how one thing caused another. There are also two time expressions in the paragraph, so you can tell that the facts are arranged in chronological order.

3. *Because, so, effect* indicate that the writer wants to show cause and effect. *In 1862* and *by the 1880s* help you see that the ideas are organized chronologically.

4. People began settling in Nebraska, the Dakotas, and the plains of Kansas.
The law pushed the native Americans off their lands.

In the paragraph, the writer makes two statements with a phrase ("Because of the law" and "A more negative effect of the law") that gives you an effect of the law.

5. (1) The second sentence tells you that an act is the same as a law.

STRATEGIES FOR SUCCESS

Example 1

Some of the supporting ideas are organized into an example. The sentence that tells you this is:

For example, a recent survey showed that a Burger King Whopper has 670 calories and gives you 40% of the protein you need in a day.

Example 2

If a person stays out in the sun too long, he or she could get sunstroke. First, get the person out of the sun and into a cool place. Then, put cool cloths or ice on the victim's skin to bring down the body temperature. Get medical help as soon as possible.

INTERPRETING WHAT YOU READ

SOMETIMES it's difficult to figure out what a writer really means. That's because writers don't always say things directly. In this unit, you will learn to "read between the lines"—to take the information the writer gives you and figure things out for yourself.

You will also learn to distinguish between fact and opinion. Writers often tell us what they think or feel. But they don't always give us the facts. It's important to be able to interpret what the writer is saying so you can form opinions of your own.

1. MAKING INFERENCES

WE make inferences every day. Suppose you hear a sportscaster say this:

"Believe it or not, folks, Harry Walker just hit a home run. Yes, I said Harry Walker—the pitcher, Harry Walker! The crowd can't believe it either!"

You are given a fact—Harry Walker just hit a home run. But the sportscaster is **implying,** or suggesting, something too. He says "believe it or not." He keeps repeating Harry's name, as if he were surprised. He says, "The crowd can't believe it either." If you think about all that information, you will probably **infer** that Harry Walker doesn't hit a home run very often.

IMPLY. To say indirectly, to suggest.

INFER. To figure out from the facts or information that is given; to read between the lines.

Writers often imply things too. They will give you certain details. But then they expect you to read between the lines. They expect you to come up with ideas or opinions of your own. Look at the next paragraph.

Mrs. Conneley lived in a tiny one-room apartment in the basement. As the doctor walked into the room, he noticed that the paint was peeling off the walls and there was no glass in the window. He pulled a chair up to the bed and took the old woman's hand.

From the information in this paragraph, what can you infer about Mrs. Conneley's economic status? Look at these details.

1. She lives in a very small apartment.
2. The paint is peeling off the walls.
3. There is no glass in the window.

This is **evidence**. From this evidence, you can infer that Mrs. Conneley is poor.

EVIDENCE. Information that proves something.

What else can you infer from the information in this paragraph? Let's look at some of the other details.

1. A doctor walks into Mrs. Conneley's room.
2. The doctor pulls a chair up to the bed and takes Mrs. Conneley's hand.
3. Mrs. Conneley is old.

The doctor pulls a chair up to the bed and takes the woman's hand. So you probably inferred that Mrs. Conneley was in bed. Add that to the other facts, and you would infer that Mrs. Conneley is sick. She might just be resting. Or the doctor might just be a friend who has come to visit. But the evidence implies that she is sick.

Actually, you have been inferring things from the beginning of this book. In Unit 2, you were asked to read the following paragraph. You had to figure out the meaning of *aviary*.

After looking at the monkeys, we decided to find the birds. We saw a big sign that said AVIARY, so we headed in that direction. When we got to the aviary, I was astounded. It was huge, and there must have been two hundred different kinds of birds inside. This was the tropical aviary. So it looked like a jungle, and the birds were every color of the rainbow.

First, you looked at the information in the paragraph. You found out that the aviary was at the zoo. It was full of birds. It looked like a jungle. You put that information together and came up with more information on your own—an aviary is probably the place in a zoo where birds are kept. In other words, you inferred what *aviary* meant from the context.

Inferring is an important reading skill. It helps you get ALL the information from a passage. It helps you get the information that is implied.

Self-Test

Answer the questions. Then compare your answers with those in *Answers and Explanations* on page 118.

Questions 1–2 are based on the following paragraph.

In the early 1800s, most factory workers worked very long hours for poor pay. Workers were often hurt or killed on the job. But in the middle of the 1800s, workers began to form unions. They asked for better pay, a shorter day, and a safer workplace. They also asked that factories stop hiring children.

Put an X next to the best answer.

1. From this paragraph, you can infer that factories in the early 1800s

   _____ (1) were clean.

   _____ (2) were unsafe.

   _____ (3) were crowded.

   _____ (4) were open all night.

   _____ (5) were dirty.

2. A "union" is probably

   _____ (1) a group of workers who work long hours for poor pay.

   _____ (2) the name for all people who work in a factory.

   _____ (3) all the workers who are hurt or killed in a factory.

   _____ (4) a group of workers who get together and try to improve working conditions.

   _____ (5) none of the above.

Questions 3–4 are based on the following paragraph.

Tom yawned, took off his reading glasses, and reached down to pick up his cane. Then he took a deep breath and pushed himself out of the chair. Every day it was harder for him to get up. And it was becoming even harder to straighten his back.

3. From the information in this paragraph, you can infer that Tom

_____ (1) is a young man.

_____ (2) is an old man.

_____ (3) is happy.

_____ (4) is healthy.

_____ (5) none of the above.

4. You can also infer that

_____ (1) Tom was reading before he decided to get up.

_____ (2) it's hard for Tom to get out of a chair.

_____ (3) Tom doesn't walk very well.

_____ (4) all of the above.

_____ (5) none of the above.

Question 5 is based on this advertisement.

5. From this ad, you can infer that

_____ (1) if your car is hard to start and it stalls, your carburetor and fuel system might be dirty.

_____ (2) if you clean the dirt, gum, and varnish out of your carburetor and fuel line, your car won't use as much gas.

_____ (3) if you use GUMOUT, your car will start more easily and it won't stall.

_____ (4) all of the above.

_____ (5) none of the above.

GUMOUT

Has your car been hard to start recently? Does it stall? Is it using more gas than it should? Try GUMOUT. GUMOUT will clean out your carburetor and clean your fuel system in no time. GUMOUT attacks the dirt, gum, and varnish that build up in your carburetor and fuel line. It leaves your car running smoothly and efficiently!

Questions 6–7 are based on the following paragraph.

Jackie Lindley gets up at 6:00 every morning so she'll have time to get breakfast for her kids and get them off to the day-care center before she goes to work. At 5:30, she picks them up and heads home to cook dinner. After dinner, she plays with the kids or reads to them. Then she gives them a bath and puts them to bed. This has been her routine for the past two years.

6. From the information in this paragraph, you can infer that Jackie Lindley

_____ (1) is probably happily married.

_____ (2) is probably a single parent.

_____ (3) has probably never been married.

_____ (4) has probably been married a very short time.

_____ (5) none of the above.

7. You can also infer that

_____ (1) Jackie Lindley is a responsible person.

_____ (2) Jackie Lindley's children are too young to go to school.

_____ (3) Jackie Lindley is a very happy woman.

_____ (4) both 1 and 2.

_____ (5) both 2 and 3.

2. DRAWING CONCLUSIONS

DRAWING **conclusions** or **concluding** involves inferring. First you have to look at the information that you have—the details the writer gives you and the details you can infer. You put them all together and think about what they mean. Then you use your logic to take one more step. You draw a conclusion. Look at this passage. What can you conclude about Billy?

DRAW A CONCLUSION, CONCLUDE. To decide something based on facts and on logic.

> Billy came out of the barn and waddled toward the pond. When he got to the edge, he flapped his wings, gave a quack, and hopped into the water. Paul Murray laughed and went back to fixing his tractor.

Look at the facts and inferences.

1. Billy has wings. (fact)
2. He waddles. (fact)
3. He quacks. (fact)
4. He likes water. (inference)

Draw your conclusion: Your logic tells you that if Billy has wings, waddles, quacks, and likes water, he must be a duck. This is the only logical conclusion about Billy you can draw.

Here is another example. What can you conclude about the surface temperature of the planet Pluto?

> The planets in our solar system are Mercury, Venus, Earth, Mars, Jupiter, Saturn, Uranus, Neptune, and Pluto. Here they are listed according to their distance from the sun. Mercury is the closest, Venus next, Earth next, etc. The closer a planet is to the sun, the hotter it is. The surface temperature of Mercury can be 625°F, while the surface temperature of Mars goes down to −191°F.

Look at the facts.

1. The planets are listed according to their distance from the sun.
2. Mercury is the closest to the sun.
3. The closer a planet is to the sun, the hotter it is.

Draw your conclusion: Putting 1 and 2 together, your logic tells you that Pluto must be the farthest planet from the sun. Adding the information in 3, you have to conclude that Pluto is the coldest planet.

Now look at this paragraph. What can you conclude?

> **Until recently, people fantasized about discovering life on Mars or Venus. Many believed there really was a "man in the moon." Now we know that only one planet in our solar system can support life. There is only one that has all the necessary conditions for life to develop.**

Look at the facts.

1. The writer tells you that there is only one planet in our solar system that can support life.
2. You know from your own experience and knowledge that there is life on Earth.

Draw your conclusion: You can conclude that Earth is the only planet in our solar system that supports life.

*F*OR YOUR INFORMATION

On an exam, you will probably never have to distinguish between making an inference and drawing a conclusion. If a question asks what you can infer or conclude from a passage, it's asking you about information that is not stated directly.

Self-Test

Answer the questions. Then compare your answers with those in *Answers and Explanations* on page 118.

Question 1 is based on the following paragraph.

If you're planning a trip south of the equator, think before you pack your suitcase. In the Southern Hemisphere, the seasons are reversed. In places like Rio de Janeiro, Brazil, Christmas comes right in the middle of summer. July is the coldest month of the year.

Put an X next to the best answer.

1. From the information in this paragraph, you can conclude that
   _____ (1) July is the perfect month to go to the beach in Rio de Janeiro.
   _____ (2) you'll need a coat if you go to Brazil in July.
   _____ (3) it's never cold in the Southern Hemisphere.
   _____ (4) in Rio de Janeiro, it's warm in December.
   _____ (5) both 2 and 4.

Question 2 is based on this advertisement.

2. You can conclude from the advertisement that
   _____ (1) cars are usually hard to start.
   _____ (2) a carburetor is part of a car.
   _____ (3) cars always run efficiently and smoothly.
   _____ (4) both 1 and 2.
   _____ (5) both 2 and 3.

GUMOUT

Has your car been hard to start recently? Does it stall? Is it using more gas than it should? Try GUMOUT. GUMOUT will clean out your carburetor and clean your fuel system in no time. GUMOUT attacks the dirt, gum, and varnish that build up in your carburetor and fuel line. It leaves your car running smoothly and efficiently!

James Springer and his identical twin, James Lewis, were separated at birth. They were raised in different homes. They did not meet again until they were 39. When they met, they found out the following: Springer's first wife was named Linda and his second wife, Betty. Lewis has also had a wife named Betty and one named Linda. Both had a son named James Allen. And both had had a dog named Toy. Their favorite subject in high school had been math. They had both studied law enforcement after high school. They had the same hobbies and the same favorite vacation place (St. Petersburg Beach, Florida). They even smoked the same brand of cigarettes and drank the same brand of beer!

3. From the facts in this article, which of the following can you conclude?
_____ (1) All twins like dogs.
_____ (2) Identical twins are more likely to get divorced than other people.
_____ (3) There are more male twins than female twins.
_____ (4) All of the above.
_____ (5) None of the above.

4. From this article, you can conclude that
_____ (1) even though these men were raised differently, they have a lot in common.
_____ (2) twins usually name their children after themselves.
_____ (3) James Springer and James Lewis liked each other.
_____ (4) all of the above.
_____ (5) none of the above.

Drinking while pregnant could have the following effects:

1. The child could grow more slowly before and after birth. Even if the baby eats well, it may be small and thin.

2. Parts of the child's face could be malformed. (The eyes could be smaller than normal, the upper lip too narrow, the chin too small.)

3. The brain could be damaged, and the head could be smaller than normal. The child could be retarded.

4. The child's body organs might not develop right.

5. From this passage, you can conclude that

_____ (1) a baby with small eyes and a small chin has a mother who drinks.

_____ (2) a woman who drinks while she's pregnant might have a child who is not normal in some way.

_____ (3) all women who drink while they're pregnant have abnormal children.

_____ (4) all of the above.

_____ (5) none of the above.

6. From the information in the passage, you can infer that

_____ (1) pregnant women shouldn't drink.

_____ (2) children with small heads are retarded.

_____ (3) babies who don't eat well are usually retarded.

_____ (4) all of the above.

_____ (5) none of the above.

3. FACT AND OPINION

SUPPOSE you saw these two **statements** about the Big Mac. Which one would you believe?

A McDonald's Big Mac has 563 calories and gives you 60% of the protein you need in a day.

The Big Mac is the best-tasting hamburger in the world today.

You probably picked the first one because it is a **fact**. The writer can prove what he said. The second statement, however, cannot be proved. Different people like different things. Everyone is not going to agree that a Big Mac is the best-tasting hamburger around. Some will prefer the Whopper, others will prefer a Wendy's. The second statement is an **opinion**. It tells what the writer thinks.

As you saw when you read the sentences about the Big

Mac, it's possible to talk about the same thing in two different ways. Look at these two paragraphs.

Some states have already passed laws that give nonsmokers the right to have a smoke-free place to work. Why don't we have a law like that? I think it's awful that I have to breathe smoke all day. In my opinion, smoking should be prohibited in ALL public places. But until that happens, I should at least have a healthy place to work.

More and more states are now passing laws to create smoke-free areas in the workplace. These laws state that an employer must provide nonsmokers with a work area where no smoking is allowed. There are some states that are even considering banning smoking in all public places.

Both of these paragraphs talk about laws that prohibit smoking in certain places. But the paragraphs are very different. The second one gives facts about the laws. It tells you what the laws say. The information can be proved—all you have to do is read the laws.

The first paragraph gives you an opinion about the laws. It tells you how one person thinks or feels about them. Not everyone would agree with the writer. In fact, some people think just the opposite. They think that a smoker has the right to smoke wherever he or she pleases.

Sometimes there are certain words and phrases that tell you that the writer is expressing a personal opinion. *I think* is an example. Underline another phrase in the first paragraph about smoking that tells you the writer is giving an opinion.

You probably underlined *In my opinion. I believe, it seems, I feel,* and *it appears* also show that a personal opinion is being expressed.

If you don't see one of these phrases, how can you tell if you're reading a fact or an opinion? As you read, you can ask yourself these questions:

"Can this statement be proved?"

"Does everyone agree that this is true?"

If the answer to either question is "No," you are probably reading an opinion.

A person who has a strong opinion about something has a **bias** for or against it. Writers are often biased. When they put down facts, they choose words that will make the reader feel the same way they do.

BIAS. A strong feeling for or against something.

Look at this sentence:

The basketball player was tall and slim.

How do you see this person? You probably picture someone who is athletic and who is the right weight. You may even imagine that the person is attractive. But what about this sentence?

The basketball player was tall and thin.

Now you probably imagine someone who is tall but needs to gain a little weight. He's probably too tall, and doesn't weigh enough. But what about this sentence?

The basketball player was tall and skinny.

Now the person definitely seems underweight. You might even think the person is unattractive.